D0772876

THE SECRET OF THE CROWN

Also by John Fraser

THE SECRET OF THE CROWN

Canada's Affair with Royalty

JOHN FRASER

This edition published in 2012 by
House of Anansi Press Inc.
110 Spadina Avenue, Suite 801
Toronto, ON, M5V 2K4
Tel. 416-363-4343
Fax 416-363-1017
www.anansi.ca

Distributed in Canada by
HarperCollins Canada Ltd.
1995 Markham Road
Scarborough, ON, M1B 5M8
Toll free tel. 1-800-387-0117

House of Anansi Press is committed to protecting our natural environment.
As part of our efforts, the interior of this book is printed on paper that contains
100% post-consumer recycled fibres, is acid-free, and is processed chlorine-free.

16 15 14 13 12   1 2 3 4 5

Library and Archives Canada Cataloguing in Publication

Fraser, John, 1944–
The secret of the crown : Canada's affair
with royalty / John Fraser.

Includes bibliographical references and index.
ISBN 978-1-77089-035-0

1. Monarchy—Canada—History. 2. Royalists—Canada—
History. 3. Great Britain—Kings and rulers. I. Title.

FC246.M6F73 2012 320.471 C2011-904021-2

Jacket design: Alysia Shewchuk
Text design and typesetting: Alysia Shewchuk

We acknowledge for their financial support of our publishing program
the Canada Council for the Arts, the Ontario Arts Council, and the Government of
Canada through the Canada Book Fund.

Printed and bound in Canada

FOR FRIENDSHIP AND INSPIRATION,
THIS BOOK IS DEDICATED TO

Michael Valpy
Journalist, Socialist, Monarchist

and

Michael Bliss
Historian, Conservative, Republican

and in grateful memory to Georges and Pauline Vanier

TABLE OF CONTENTS

PROLOGUE

Why Secret?

"I would like to affirm before you tonight that wherever the future may take us, my admiration and affection for Canada and Canadians everywhere is, and will always remain, clear, strong and sure."

— The Queen, in Quebec during the Golden Jubilee of her Accession to the throne, 2002

THIS IS A BOOK ABOUT THE CROWN IN CANADA. As a study or polemic, it is both personal and selective. It is not a history any more than it is a constitutional treatise, although history and the constitution are crucial ingredients in the tale. Instead, it is an attempt to confirm to those who believe in the Crown in Canada why they are wise to hold on to that belief, and it is also an attempt to explain to those who "don't get it" why there are good reasons not to sacrifice the Crown on an altar of national or patriotic logic based on some aspects of contemporary (and transient) sentiment. If my account of the institution cannot win them over, so be it, but I want to say right at the beginning to such readers: thank you for hearing me out. On the other hand, it is not a book for those who see the Queen and the Royal Family as "parasites" or as hopelessly chipped heirlooms from a forgotten era. I leave them happily with their fantasies and their ignorance of our country's history and traditions.

That said, no one is more surprised to be writing such a book than myself. To write confidently any sort of positive book on the role of the monarchy in Canada a few years ago would have been almost unthinkable. Out of sheer brazen affection for the institution, the deed could have been done, but a publisher would have been hard to find. Even if such a book had seen the light of day outside of a specialty press, there was also the problem that close colleagues would have looked at me as if I had gone completely mad. (Some still will!) Like many friends of the Canadian Crown, I felt cowed by a certain kind of peer disapprobation.

Only once did I sneak my constrained admiration into hardcover. It was in another book, called *Eminent Canadians,* in which current Canadians of note were paired with their historic antecedents: Jean Chrétien with Wilfrid Laurier, for example; and the then editor-in-chief of the *Globe and Mail,* William Thorsell, with the redoubtable founder of the *Globe,* George Brown. In the last section, I wrote about Queen Elizabeth and Queen Victoria, *as Canadians.* In vain, as it turned out. Reviewers passed over the section lightly, as one might sweetly tolerate a child with an overheated imagination.

Others dismissed the effort as either weird or whimsical.

That was a big lesson for me on how far down the road to dismantling the role of the Crown in Canada we had progressed. The whole notion of the Crown seemed not so much in jeopardy as in steady, inexorable decline, and for the life of me I couldn't see how the slide could be stopped. For the most part, the self-proclaimed cognoscenti in political life and the chattering classes — the "commentariat" — had given up on it. My colleague and friend Michael Valpy of the *Globe and Mail*, to whom, along with the eminent Canadian historian Michael Bliss, this book is dedicated, was the most notable exception, but even he would agree that his fortitude in defence of the Crown over the years came at some considerable cost, both emotionally and professionally, particularly when colleagues didn't take him seriously. Believe me, he was serious, and a lot braver than I was. Our enemy was not hatred, but indifference buttressed by spurts of mockery.

Since the 1960s, successive administrations of the Canadian government had surreptitiously or sometimes even openly encouraged people to forget or snort at the Royal Family. Quietly, progressively, and often stealthily, the traditional symbols of the Queen's Canadian realm vanished: the crown icons disappeared from mailboxes and government offices; the word "royal" was removed from the branches of our armed services;[1] portraits of the Queen were removed from government offices, embassies, and other missions abroad,[2] followed by their disappearance from the country's classrooms, where many teachers reinforced the negativity by equating the Crown to our colonial past while never outlining its careful post-colonial evolution; although her profile remained on the coinage, the Sovereign's image was replaced on most of our stamps and paper currency, save for the $20 bill;[3] the Queen was rarely asked to come and preside over an opening of Parliament anymore, and when she did get invited here it was often to preside only at some further diminution of her role and status. The ludicrously named federal "Department of Canadian Heritage"

---

[1]   Removed, that is, until they were restored to the Royal Canadian Navy and the Royal Canadian Air Force forty-three years later, in 2011, by the Tory administration of Stephen Harper — an event which alternately delighted or perplexed Canadians.

[2]   Also restored, in October 2011, by order of the Minister of Foreign Affairs. It is very difficult to write an up-to-date book on the Canadian Crown when almost every other day the government announces yet another change to the storyline!

[3]   Now, ironically, thanks to inflation, the Queen's face on the $20 bill is more familiar than Sir Wilfrid Laurier's on the $5 bill or Sir John A. Macdonald's on the $10 bill, who were clearly intended to have pride of position over the Sovereign when the changed portraits were first ordered up in 1969. *Sic transit gloria economica!*

was given control over the image of the Canadian Royal Family and systematically downgraded it in order to build up the notion that the appointed governor general of Canada was the real head of state. Soon enough, the governors general began to believe it and even declare it, denying the mystical remnants of potency remaining in the office after a succession of banal political appointments, from the dull-witted (Ed Schreyer) to the sweetly benighted (Roméo LeBlanc).

This gradual attrition was working. By the time the twentieth century had turned into the twenty-first, the federal establishment of the country had us well down the road to an undeclared republic. As Michael Bliss often enough said, "It (the monarchy) doesn't mean anything to most young Canadians. It will die a natural death at the same time as the dwindling band of oldsters who still support it die off too." This line had a certain seemingly evident logic to it, but it annoyed me enormously because it wasn't something that had to happen. Canadians were too good-natured to understand some of the incremental deviousness and stealth of a bureaucracy like that at the Department of Canadian Heritage (it's better today because it has new orders and new civil servants who are actually civil), or the Prime Minister's Office, or even the Rideau Hall office of the governor general.

In truth, I always preferred the straightforward honesty of republican advocates like Bliss, *Globe and Mail* columnist Jeffrey Simpson, or the Canadian cabinet minister John Manley, who openly called for the end of the monarchy in this country. (Although Manley surely merited the Boor of the Year Award in 2002 for pontificating publicly about his particular distaste for the monarchy on the eve of escorting the Queen as her minister-in-attendance on a royal tour.) Boorishness aside, these republican sympathizers openly make their points, many of which are cogent in a certain context. Still, it always amazes me that they never fully take in what they are throwing away, concentrating as they do on the alleged absurdities, with hardly a nod at the reality.

Clearly, though, they were also resonating with a significant part of the population, and the defence of the Crown was left to an ad hoc group of provincial lieutenant governors' offices (notably those of Ontario, Saskatchewan, Nova Scotia, and Newfoundland) and small organizations like the Monarchist League of Canada or the Friends of the Canadian Crown, which worked valiantly to rally the cause and sound alarms, but also sometimes — and inadvertently — made the republican case through arch-fussiness about small details while overlooking the main points.

As the Blisses or Simpsons rarely failed to point out, there was a timely logic about it all. The *Globe and Mail*, for example, once such a staunch believer in the constitutional monarchy, came out editorially in favour of establishing a Republic of Canada once the Queen dies.[4] There was residual respect everywhere for the aging Queen, and not many Canadians wanted her discomforted. The self-evident fact that she had done such a good job for over half a century, justifying her role time and again in the Canadian scheme of things, somehow was ignored or dismissed out of hand. Logic collapsed: *Queen Elizabeth has done a great job for Canada; therefore let's make sure there is no monarchy when she dies.*

The lynchpin in this strategy of waiting till the Sovereign was dead — admittedly somewhat haunted for republicans by the alarming spectacle of longevity amongst the women of the House of Windsor (the Queen, in her mid-eighties, still has a way to go to surpass her mother, who made it to over one hundred) — was the much-espoused ridiculousness of her heir, the Prince of Wales, ever becoming "King of

---

4   This was under the editorship of William Thorsell in the 1990s. His successor, John Stackhouse, has reversed this editorial decision, and the *Globe and Mail* is once again, on the subject of the monarchy, a supporter of the constitutional status quo.

Canada." Inevitably, the more polite faction amongst republicans would conclude their arguments, either seriously or satirically, by evoking the "absurdity" of Prince Charles. His "jug-ears" often had a role to play in the argument, as well as his inappropriate behaviour in talking out loud about what, in his opinion, was wrong in the world. And then there were his "bizarre" causes, from alternative medicine to decrying the evil inherent in most modern architecture.

The assumption that the heir is unsuitable still resonates and, in debate, seems to make the republican point more strongly than arguments such as Canada's being a mature country with no need of kings and queens, or having an inherent majesty in its own history and geography that makes kings and queens superfluous, or — most simply — of being an independent nation, a place of opportunity where hereditary rights are nonsensical, unfair, and wholly unnecessary. Nope! Forget all that. Did you hear what Prince Charles said to Camilla on his cellphone?

We enjoy embracing the gossip and forgetting the reality. There's a wee problem, though. Even amongst intelligent and coherent republicans, only the vaguest of concepts exist of how to get rid of the monarchy, even if the day should come when there is a collective will to do so. That's because constitutionally there really isn't an easy way, short of parliamentary fiat. Thanks to the constitutional arrangements worked out back in 1981–82 between the provinces and the Liberal administration of Pierre Trudeau, there would have to be total unanimity among the provinces for Canada to become a republic. So technically it can be done, but it is hugely unlikely to happen.

At the very least, even if all the English-speaking legislatures agreed to go along with the idea (and just imagining the government of Newfoundland or Prince Edward Island or Saskatchewan or Nova Scotia consenting is a real stretch), the one province where it is assumed that the strongest anti-monarchical feelings exist — Quebec — would inevitably move to block such a move. It's so easy to predict, I wonder why people don't get it. The reason why? Because any change of the constitutional status quo that does not deal with issues more pertinent to the Canadian relationship with Quebec — such as aboriginal legal and land settlements or spiralling shared costs on health care — will always be defeated by a Quebec administration. So ask yourself this: what federal government in the foreseeable future is going to tackle the issue of Quebec before the issue of the monarchy?[5] Or, if you prefer it the other way around, what federal government is going to tackle the issue of the monarchy before settling the constitutional anomalies that persist in its relationship with Quebec? Take your choice: they are both self-answering questions.

On top of all that, look at the useful Australian experience. In 1999, the government of Australia held a referendum on the future of their version of a monarchy (same cast, different locale). Despite polling that clearly showed the majority of Australians felt it was time to sever links to the Crown, the referendum showed otherwise. Why? Sudden angst over leaving the mother-monarch? Not at all. Australians suddenly woke up to the fact that their prime minister, or any prime minister of the day, was going to be given additional powers to determine a redefined head of state, and this was seen as undermining and diminishing regional authority. It also turned out that sticking with the system already in place seemed a safer bet than branching out, and that

---

5   And then there's Prime Minister Jean Chrétien's typically pungent defence of the monarchy through his interpretation of French-Canadian history: "When you think about it," he said in 1994, "the American Revolution was promoted by the French. And they, Quebec, refused to join. It was nothing to do with language but a lot to do with religion. And they felt more secure in the main, Catholics in Canada. More security for the religion, what the monarchy was giving them in those days, compared to the Americans. So they stayed."

one of the central reasons for preserving the Crown is to make sure that there is some sort of check on the growing power of the Prime Minister's Office.

Still, "better the devil known than unknown" is not exactly a rallying cry that resonates *a mari usque ad mare*,[6] and if the Crown is to survive in Canada — and not just survive but also thrive — we have to do better than that. I had always believed that the two strongest arguments for retention of the Crown were: it exists and it works. I still believe only fools start tinkering around with things that work, but I have sadly come to realize that there is no accounting for fools: sometimes, they even get elected and cause great damage.

And then, just recently, a sequence of events has led directly to *The Secret of the Crown*. Against all odds, and thanks to a minority government that was not hell-bent on diminishing the role of the Crown, "adjustments" (i.e., staff changes) were made at the Department of Canadian Heritage, resulting in the Queen and Prince Philip's hugely successful tour of the country, highlighted by a superb Canada Day celebration on Parliament Hill. That was on July 1, 2010.

---

6   That's the Latin motto of Canada on all our official coats of arms. It's from Psalm 72 (verse 8) of the Jewish scriptures: *"He shall have dominion also from sea to sea and from the river unto the ends of the earth."* It was approved and proclaimed by King George V in November 1921.

Shortly afterwards, I got involved in a caper that saw me debating the monarchy with a dear friend and Massey College colleague, the aforementioned and outstanding Canadian historian Michael Bliss. For reasons that still mystify me, but which I respect, he is a passionate republican, and because of that I was vaguely worried about losing my cool and rupturing the close friendship my wife and I have with him and his wife, a friendship that goes all the way back to the 1960s, when he was my wife's history teacher at Lawrence Park Collegiate in north Toronto.

The debate was the first of four on historical Canadian themes, and they were all designed to be instantly provocative, at least in the way the organizers touted them. One debated the notion that Canada was right to hang the iconic Métis leader Louis Riel in 1885; another attacked multiculturalism; a third posited that Pierre Trudeau was the worst prime minister in our history. Bliss and I were to debate the role of the Crown on a resolution that it was high time to wind down the monarchy in Canada and put the Royal Family in metaphorical tumbrils. The setting was the grand concourse of the Royal Ontario Museum and nearly a thousand people turned up. That was the first shock. Much as I used to despair about the role of the Crown in Canada, I worried more about the lethargic decency of Canadians. People didn't seem to hate the Crown or the Royal Family; they just didn't care to do anything to support it. This lethargy was now reinforced with a couple of generations of willfully induced ignorance.

To my amazement, just the announcement of the debate started creating real buzz, and when I arrived at the *Royal* Ontario Museum in the heart of Toronto, still known as the *Queen City*, I was truly shocked. This was one lively crowd. As the debate unfolded, Bliss and I went at it, relatively politely, and in the end I won by about a sixty-to-forty vote. However, Bliss won the waverers[7] and he was particularly strong at the end of the debate, when he played the Prince Charles gambit. We both emerged from the exercise fairly pleased with ourselves, but I was left with a profoundly nagging feeling that I had let my side down.

I admire Professor Bliss's passion. I always have, and that passion is what has sustained him through the writing of so many wonderful books on Canadian history. I felt that I had a similar passion for my side of the

---

7   The organizers took a vote at the beginning of each debate: those for and against the motion, and those who were reserving their opinion until they heard the arguments. I held the majority of those who voted pro-monarchy at the beginning, but Bliss won the majority of those who hadn't initially decided.

debate, as did many Canadians, but I never showed it. I never fought our corner openly, I always worried about being mocked, I was shy to the point of negligence and thus complicit, in my own special way, to the diminution of the Crown. So another reason for this book is an attempt to remedy that fault of inhibition in myself.

Like many defenders of the Crown, I had "educated" myself not to make too much of a fuss, for fear that it might bring the whole fragile edifice tumbling down. I should have had more faith in our cause because, as it turns out, it has far more supporters than I imagined. Not only that, but once you got people to think beyond the *scandale du jour* (say, who was sucking Fergie's toes, or who her ex-husband, Prince Andrew, was courting) and take a serious look at the issue of a constitutional monarchy set in the northern half of North America, you could make a reasonable or even a very good case for it, and I was grateful for the chance to try.

And then, in short order, there was the huge success of the royal wedding between Prince William and Catherine Middleton, and almost immediately afterwards it was announced that their first tour as a married couple would be to Canada, "the senior of Her Majesty's realms."

And glimmering in the immediate distance was the Diamond Jubilee of Queen Elizabeth herself — only the second such celebration of a sixty-year reign in Canadian history — and a chance to celebrate one of the most extraordinary human beings of our own time, and the time of our parents and grandparents, and the time of our children and grandchildren. A woman whose father was held in the arms of Queen Victoria and who, in all likelihood, will hold in her own arms a great-grandchild who, with loyalty and luck, will also be a sovereign of Canada.[8] That's a picture to wait for, because it will embody a stretch of our history from the early nineteenth century to quite possibly the beginning of the twenty-second century.

So here lies the main goal this book hopes to accomplish: to show that we are part of a lucky continuum that gives definition and continuity to our beloved country and puts us in a very special historical pathway that has protected us constitutionally over such a long period of time. That continuum, the Canadian Crown, also has the power, if we let it, to reign in our imaginations as well. The royal and viceregal individuals involved in this centuries-old tale are fun to write and speculate about, but they are not nearly as important as the reality they represent. It is at the heart of the great secret

---

[8]   I am talking about a future child of Prince William and the Duchess of Cambridge, in case my genealogical enthusiasm is confusing you.

of the Crown in Canada today: we are what we choose to be, and we are a country mature enough to carry our history forward with us, not abandon it; to correct mistakes from the past; and to build upon what has been useful to us.

This is a destiny that will always be challenging Canadians. When we say "God Bless the Queen," we are really saying "God Bless Us." We are also saying "God Bless Canada."

John Fraser
Split Rock Island, Georgian Bay
Massey College, Toronto
Labour Day, 2011

CHAPTER ONE

The Marriage of a Prince

*Le Canada est une monarchie constitutionnelle.
Depuis 1534, date de la prise de possession du
Canada par le roi de France, l'histoire de notre
pays a été marquée par le règne d'une succession
ininterrompue de souverains, tant français que
britanniques, qui ont eu une influence continue
sur le développement de notre pays.*[9]

— From "Le Canada, une monarchie constitutionnelle," an
illustrated brochure published by the Senate of Canada.

---

*A Quebec politician has called Prince William
and his wife, Catherine, "parasites" for visiting
Canada on the taxpayers' dime. "The taxpayers
should not pay for that," Amir Khadir, who represents Montreal's Mercier riding for the Quebec
Solidaire party, told reporters, referring to the
newlyweds' impending visit. "Do you want your
taxes used for a Royal couple?"*

— From the *National Post,* June 1, 2011

---

9   *"Canada is a constitutional monarchy. Since 1534, when the king of
France claimed possession of what is now Canada, the history of our country has been marked by the reigns of an uninterrupted succession of monarchs, both French and British, who have had a significant influence on our
country's development."*

LET US BEGIN WITH A HAPPY EVENT, THE MARRIAGE of a prince. In 1867, in his seminal study of the English constitution, Walter Bagehot wrote: "A princely marriage is the brilliant edition of a universal fact, and as such, it rivets mankind." And so it was again nearly a century and a half later. On the night before his wedding in April 2011, young Prince William went out amongst his people. They had been camping for hours on the grassy verges near his home at Clarence House, a block away from the ur-abode of all royalty, Buckingham Palace. Some were erecting tents; others had makeshift shawls around their shoulders to stave off a drop in temperature. The kids were restless. There was a threat of rain and all night long to wait. And then, just like that, there he was, a little touch of William in the night.

"Take care, guys," he said, and "keep warm" and "thanks for your support." Someone asked if he was nervous. "I just have to get my lines right," he said.

Well, it wasn't Prince Hal and it wasn't Shakespearean — "guys" was the big giveaway — but it resonated nevertheless. A King in the making, a husband on the cusp, a new duke (of Cambridge) about to be minted: William Arthur Philip Louis showed he had the common touch, just as his bride-to-be was about to show the world how flawlessly she could cross the line between commoner and future queen. At the centre point of both journeys, which was where they met on their wedding day, a new story was about to begin.

It was also an important moment in royal chronology, and if you are one of those for whom history, romance, majesty, and constitutional sanity reign supreme, this glorious wedding, which went off without a hitch, was also — to quote the preacher of the day — a moment of hope. If, on the other hand, the whole exercise seemed too silly for words, well, this was not your day and the only parade the rain fell on was yours.

The elegant nuptials of Canada's future King and Queen (and Britain's too, and fourteen other realms that have been happy to embrace their storied pasts and make them work for their futures) had been rehearsed to the last tiny detail, and it all paid off. Kings and queens and crown princesses came to the Abbey; the Syrian ambassador

was disinvited; a couple of former British prime ministers (Tony Blair and Gordon Brown) never made the cut;
Canada's prime minister, Stephen Harper, had to decline
in order to fight for his Tory administration in an upcoming federal election; Elton John came with his fussy man
(not liking their seats, he demanded better ones); Anglican
nuns who minister to the homeless sat in the sanctuary
beside the future King and Queen; uniquely, some vacant
valet/varlet let the newly appointed Canadian governor
general, David Johnston, wear a bizarre outfit resembling
white-tie evening dress, perhaps the better to stand out
amongst the properly attired.

And that's to mention just a few of the two thousand
who got inside Westminster Abbey. Outside, a million
people turned out to line the streets, and somewhere between one and two billion people (give or take a dozen)
around the world tuned in. The threatened rain stayed
away and sunshine emerged from behind the storm
clouds at precisely the right moments, filling the ancient
precincts with talismans of warmth, enlivening even
the ghostly effigies and tombs of so many of William's
ancestors, all gathered metaphysically around to cheer
him on his way.

As for the never-again-to-be Ms. Catherine Elizabeth
Middleton, who had waited seven long years to get her

man to the altar, she was not only beautiful to behold, she also exuded the calm and dignified aura that has so bewitched her growing legion of admirers. On that first day of her new title, she proved to be a duchess to trump all duchesses. When the bearded Bishop of London, the Right Reverend Richard Chartres, began his brief and eloquent homily with a quote from St. Catherine of Siena, whose feast day it was, it was surely mostly directed her way: "Be who God meant you to be," he quoted the saint as saying, "and you will set the world on fire."

She was doing that from the first moment she appeared at the Abbey door with her father, looking solemnly, and perhaps appropriately, nervous. The combined choirs of Westminster Abbey sang Sir Charles Hubert Parry's stirring setting of the 122nd Psalm, "I was glad when they said unto me, I will go into the house of the Lord," and before the three-minute walk down a tree-festooned nave aisle was half concluded, you knew everything was going to be fine. The bride was in control in a stunning gown, which, like the floral decorations and beautiful music of the service, was understated and hauntingly simple. The groom himself had set the tone when he arrived with his brother and best man, Prince Harry, forty minutes before the ceremony began and did what all nervous grooms do: pretended not to be nervous and spoke to some of the relatives.

The other hirsute prelate, the Archbishop of Canterbury, the Most Reverend Rowan Williams, led the couple through their actual marriage vows, using a slightly reformed service from the Anglican Church's Book of Common Prayer. The bride, having promised to love and cherish Prince William in sickness and in health, for better or for worse, and up to the very moment of death, wisely eschewed the vow "to obey." Many senior members of William's family, only a few feet away, who had come to rue that particular vow — like his uncle (Prince Andrew) and his aunt (Princess Anne, the "Princess Royal") — would not have objected.

As the Bishop of London pointed out, all couples at their marriage service go through a transformation. It was a measure of the affection felt for these two young and beautiful people that family and clergy actually let them have a service that was so comprehensively focused on them, right down to their own prayer, which was read out at the end of the homily:

"God our Father, we thank you for our families; for the love that we share and for the joy of our marriage. In the busyness of each day, keep our eyes fixed on what is real and important in life and help us to be generous with our time and love and energy. Strengthened by our union, help us to serve and comfort those who suffer . . ."

There is more than an echo in these words of his grandmother's pledge to the Commonwealth sixty-four years earlier, in 1947, just before her own marriage: "I declare before you that my whole life, be it long or short, shall be devoted to your service." Not once has she ever hinted at veering one degree from that solemn oath, not even during her famous *annus horribilis*, when three of her four children's marriages collapsed and her favourite domicile, Windsor Castle, was badly damaged in a fire. Even then, she never flinched from her sense of public duty. Even then, to use the language of her blunt spouse, Prince Philip, she "just got on with it."

Perhaps that's why at the wedding of her grandson who is carrying the future of the throne she has so carefully tried to nurture and protect, the Queen herself seemed so clearly happy and, as usual, in total control of her tightly held emotions. "Duty" has not been the byword of her times, however faithful she has been to it as a guiding principle, so she must have felt some sense of relief that all was going so well.

The same could be said for the beleaguered father of the groom, the Prince of Wales, the heir to the throne, who consistently for the past couple of decades has been dealt a bad press and a troubling image. Yet it was under Charles's aegis at Clarence House that the biggest single coup of this marriage was pulled off, one that offers a major breakthrough in our understanding and appreciation of monarchy. Although they were late and slow learners, Prince Charles's team found a way in preparing and planning for this wedding to override the more merciless members of the anti-royalist media. This is the same media — much of it owned by the Prince of Media Darkness, Rupert Murdoch — that has been such a relentless plague in the Prince of Wales's own life and indeed on the well-being of the throne itself.

Inspiring and moving as the service was, and however impeccable the security arrangements and the spirit of the day, the story of how Clarence House and Buckingham Palace quietly, almost surreptitiously, beat the snoopy and cruder members of the media at their own game has become increasingly apparent. Keeping the groom's stag party and the bride's dress secret till the moment they no longer needed to be kept secret were simply talismans of the newly savvy monarchy — small but widely noticed victories in a far bigger game. No one at the Palace or Clarence House felt the need to attack all the errors or outright lies reported in the old media: the new royal media simply flew above it.

IT IS NOW widely acknowledged that this wedding was Twittered and Facebooked for all it was worth, and this has been a huge success, parallel to the massive broadcasting of the wedding itself. It has given ordinary people a chance to get past all the intermediaries and directly embrace that sense of magic and mystery that used to support the monarchy when only our imaginations and a few Movietone clips at the local cinema were available.

Walter Bagehot, that already cited nineteenth-century pontificator of the role of the Crown, also said that the allure of monarchy fades the more it is exposed to the light of day. Well, Bagehot did not foresee twenty-first-century celebrity culture. He thought the decline of deference would lead to a lessening of monarchy's hold on our imaginations, and to some extent that has been true. On the other hand, the precipitous rise of the absurd world of instant celebrity has certainly induced contempt for the more superficial members of royalty, but at the same time it has enhanced by its very superficiality the more grounded celebrity of the Queen. It's a curious turn of events, but real nonetheless.

If celebrity monarchy is often a trial for those who support the monarchy for constitutional and historical reasons, then it still feeds into the business: that's business as in mystique and altruism at the high end of the equation, and business as in garbagey gossip at the other end. The obvious "disaster story" the Royal Family apparently has no ability to control is the divorced Duchess of York, Sarah Ferguson. She and her ex-husband, Prince Andrew, Duke of York, have been media fodder for years, with no sign of a let-up.

Sarah — or, more media-familiarly, "Fergie" — was not invited to The Wedding. Her daughters came, of course. They are heirs to the throne. They are grandchildren of the Queen. They are also from the womb and loins of The Inappropriate Ones, and staying true to the DNA, they came in the most fascinating and arch "fascinators" ever made — so fascinating they made them the laughingstock of a couple of billion watchers around the world, and then the fascinators became so famously fascinating that they were auctioned off for a lot of loot to charity. The owners of the heads upon which the fascinators were so perilously perched were seated next to their father, Prince Andrew, seemingly hovering for protection behind his mother the Queen, hovering because he was still in disgrace for his own *liaisons-complètement-folles* — fancy girls and pornographers et cetera.

Both of Catherine's siblings also got it in the neck almost the next day after their sister's global nuptials.

That's when the "lesser" media (duly reported upon by the "higher media") published some private photographs of the two (sold by "friends") in vaguely risqué poses. The mean-spirited trafficking of the photos was, of course, completely unfair and proof of how fickle friendship can be, but it also provided graphic evidence, if any was needed, of the price to be paid for such close proximity to royalty. The particular victims of that proximity also serve a dark purpose, like scarecrows in a farmer's field.

Royal scarecrows — for that is what they are — seem to be part of the package in Great Britain. A scarecrow does just that: scares crows away from what they are really after — the newly sown crops. Human scarecrows divert human crows (Mr. Murdoch's team of scandal-mongering journalists, for example) away from important things (say, the role of the Crown in contemporary society, which is always a legitimate area of inquiry, pro or con). Human scarecrows also serve to instruct the wider public in comfortable home truths, such as: there's a price to be paid for wealth and prestige, or being royal isn't all it's cracked up to be, or . . . well, supply your own cliché.

Throughout every reign, there's been a royal scarecrow to divert a certain type of attention from the Sovereign and focus our minds on what actually counts in Crown and Country: gossip, scandal, and — above all — inappropriateness. The divorced Duchess of York is only the latest to be served up to the cause, but she may yet prove to be the most successful yet.[10] So it was once for the "bossy-boots" and "Germanic" Princess Michael of Kent till Fergie came along, or "the spoiled and selfish" Princess Margaret till Princess Michael of Kent came along. So it's going to be for Prince Harry, wonderful sparky spirit that he nevertheless is. This spirit will be turned around and held against him eventually, although he looks to be one of the most resourceful royal figures in years. The people who inhabit the close margins of royalty, unless they are very quiet and lead almost monastic lives, are sitting ducks. Well, either sitting ducks or useful scarecrows.

In Canada, where we leave it to ex–prime ministers to walk off with curiously obtained cash, we are usually spared the problems of the lesser members of the Royal Family. For the most part, Canada's Royal Family consists of precisely four people: the Queen, Prince Philip, Prince Charles, and Prince William. The rest of the Family Firm have connections to various Canadian

---

[10]   The only time this didn't work was for King Edward VIII, but then he made the catastrophic mistake of marrying his scarecrow, Wallis Simpson.

institutions, but Canada has been able to transform the British monarchy into the Canadian "Crown," and it's about the niftiest constitutional trick we have ever pulled off: Monarchy Lite, royalty without scarecrows, the Crown Convenient.[11] We take on the good and the bad of the lesser members of the Royal Family as we see fit or are interested, but it is not at all the same as it is for the British, who will relish gossip about almost anything that crawls and has a title.

The obverse side of the usefulness of scarecrows for unworthy reasons is the usefulness of scarecrows for worthy reasons. That's because they also allow a contrasting reinforcement in the public's mind of the Queen's own rigid sense of public duty: unswerving, unyielding, unsullied, and unmatched in her own long

---

[11]   To truly appreciate the difference between the Canadian and British Crowns, a comparison of parliamentary state openings is useful. When the Queen has opened a session of the Canadian Parliament, she is accompanied by no more than four officials and often is dressed in normal civvies. In the "Mother of Parliaments" in London, she comes crowned and robed, four pageboys carry her train, and her attendants include the Lord Chancellor, the Lord Chamberlain, the Comptroller of the Lord Chamberlain's Office (who has to keep his or her eye on the Imperial State Crown), the Earl Marshal of England (the Duke of Norfolk), the Assistant Comptroller of the Chamberlain's Office (who carries the "Cap of Maintenance" — look it up for yourself, as this footnote is already too long by half), a minimum of four Gentlemen Ushers, the Sovereign's "Serjeants-at-Arms" with their maces, and two lines of dismounted troopers of the Household Calvary.

lifetime. That's worth considering the next time you shake your head in disbelief and chuckle as Fergie pours out her screwed-up heart to Oprah Winfrey. That contrast also underscores another salient point about celebrity and monarchy, because it is tied directly to the fleeting nature of celebrity status.

In his book *On Royalty,* Jeremy Paxman wrote that "royalty and mass media are made for each other." Royalty, he argued, is based on "mystery" and the media is based on "disclosure," and the Royal Family has such a deeply ambivalent relationship to its celebrity status because it can't abide it but also can't do without it. "Courtiers may harrumph at what they claim to be impertinence," Paxman writes, "but no modern monarchy can survive without the connivance of the newspapers and television. They are the amniotic fluid of royalty."

In fact, in the wake of the crisis that engulfed the Family Firm when Prince Charles's marriage imploded publicly in 1992, culminating in Princess Diana's death in a Paris traffic tunnel five years later, a wiser and far more adroit team of media handlers has discovered, and embraced, a new way of circumventing Paxman's thesis, which was not wrong but is now dated.

Go to your favourite search engine, for example, and ask it to find you an eight-minute clip of Princess Anne, the Princess Royal, discussing the kidnapping attempt that happened on the Mall in 1974. You will hear something far more eloquent and powerful than anything any journalist could possibly write about Anne's courage and quick wit. In fact, you will learn more about this extraordinary and underestimated woman than anything short of personal acquaintance could possibly provide. She pinpointed, indirectly, the total uselessness of celebrity status for a member of the Royal Family in danger or duress when she recounted the absurd moment — a minute or so after a lone police officer had been shot and wounded and the would-be kidnapper, with two revolvers, had entered her limousine — when a pedestrian out for a stroll on the Mall sauntered over for a little look-see. Peering inside the beleaguered vehicle, he said, "Hm! So it is," and then resumed his pleasant promenade. It was around this time (it took close to a quarter of an hour for police reinforcements to arrive, although they were only a few metres from Buckingham Palace), Princess Anne noted, that the back of her dress ripped right across and threatened to fall off her front. "And that," she said with a steely grin, "was [my assailant's] most dangerous moment!"

So do yourself a favour and watch this clip on your own because it offers a genuine insight into a reality most people never see, and it also highlights how part of the success of Prince William's marriage to Catherine Middleton and the subsequent royal tour of Canada was the ability of ordinary people to get beyond the traditional coverage.

The largely unquoted masses found a way of partaking in the tour without intermediaries, through various websites, but especially the monarchy's own website and the one set up by the Department of Canadian Heritage. At the same time it was equally intriguing watching the coverage of the Canada Day proceedings on Parliament Hill courtesy of Peter Mansbridge and the Canadian Broadcasting Corporation.

I love the Canadian Broadcasting Corporation and I really respect Peter Mansbridge, but both it and he were caught out badly on their Canada Day coverage. It was embarrassing and often painful to see such poor preparation, and that the usually resourceful and eloquent Mansbridge had constantly to resort to a former editor of *Hello Canada* to bridge the gulf of his ignorance. Her English accent was simply inappropriate, while the resulting patter was silly and often inappropriate, confirming that the thinking heads at the CBC did not understand what was unfolding before their eyes. They all bought into the idea of "two foreign celebrities" somehow being part of the Canada Day show and missed, almost entirely, the historic importance of the moment — and also the political mileage the Conservative administration was gaining.

Immediately prior to the CBC's coverage on Parliament Hill of the Canada Day proceedings, CTV's coverage of the evocative and moving citizenship ceremony across the river at the Museum of Civilization was straightforward and eloquent. They were clever enough to focus on the uniqueness of the occasion and to understand that the stars of the show were not just William and Catherine but all the new Canadians swearing their oaths to Crown and Country.[12]

The fact that the usually well-briefed Mansbridge knew so little about the Crown in Canada and also missed the first major manifestation of the success of the royal tour was not as much disheartening as it was further proof, if it was needed, that there is a

---

[12]   In striking contrast, CTV hired Richard Berthelsen, who is a former private secretary to the lieutenant governor of Ontario and has also worked at Rideau Hall. Berthelsen knew his stuff backwards, spoke sensibly and eloquently about all aspects of the royal visit, and made sure viewers understood the relevant history, protocol, and significance of the unfolding events. He was a star.

generational discomfort with the monarchy. I believe that this discomfort is limited to some members of the generation that stopped looking for the deeper well-springs of loyalty and national longing beyond Expo 67 and centennial year (and the Quiet Revolution in Quebec, for that matter). That the Canadian monarchy still have the capacity to stir people who don't feel they have to give up an iota of pride in Canada, but see in the constitutional monarchy a solid buttress for Canadian identity and an unambiguous and apolitical means of supporting national values of service and commitment, must be a shock for some members of that generation.

This makes contemporary monarchists quite different from the "tribal monarchists" of the past. I should know. I used to be a tribal monarchist, but that was in 1953, in the twilight of the British Empire. You didn't have to question such things in those days. "God Save the King" and later "God Save the Queen" were played before every civic, provincial, or federal event of significance. They were played in theatres and movie houses and sporting arenas. The Sovereign as symbol of national pride was not much questioned. Her picture was on our coinage and paper currency, in all our classrooms and in all government offices, federal or provincial. "God

THE SECRET OF THE CROWN

Save the Queen" and "O Canada" were played at the end of the broadcasting day on all Canadian stations.

When all this started to change, when automatic deference ended, when our historians and our school-teachers started to alter the educational materials and traditional storylines, it became a kind of Canadian logic that the monarchy would automatically dwindle and then just disappear. This didn't give due credit to the institution's ability to survive, and although its diminished status is quite tangible, nevertheless the resurgence of sequestered emotional support for the Crown that has been a-building over several years proves the institution's durability.

But the durability of the Crown is no longer built on deference or tribal siren calls. British heritage doesn't mean much anymore in Canada, even to those who have it. When anti-monarchists cite the diminishing appeal of the British connection to attack the Crown in Canada, they are way wide of the contemporary mark. Most young people don't even know what the Soviet Union was, let alone the British Empire.

So the world doesn't stand still, for colonists or revolutionaries, for monarchists or republicans, for anyone. Yet the Crown endures in Canada. Inexplicably so to some people inside and outside the country. "It surpasses understanding," wrote the former Labour Party cabinet minister and now life peer Lord (Andrew) Adonis, "that Canada or Australia would still want a head of state from another country." The British novelist Will Self feels that the monarchy "infantalises"[13] Britons and — for different reasons — this is felt by a number of Canadians too, especially if a royal tour becomes hugely successful. Successful royal tours drive them almost berserk.

That's why this wedding has been such good news. It promises a continuation of the magic, the mystery, and the stabilizing civil solution to our fractious political propensities. Quietly accompanying the royal nuptials was the implicit assurance that we would be spared the rancour and divisiveness of any of the constitutional alternatives.

---

[13] Self, like a number of upper-middle-class Britons of a certain hue (Oxford educated, he is the son of a London School of Economics professor and married, the first time, the granddaughter of Lord Hylton and the great-granddaughter of H. H. Asquith, the British prime minister), decries the monarchy because of its reinforcement of class values: "Post-Diana," he wrote in the April 2011 issue of the British magazine *Prospect*, "the Windsors are the foremost example of people who are feted in the media for accidental reasons, and not by virtue of any talent, let alone determination to succeed. People unconsciously understand this: for them, marrying into the Windsors is the genealogical equivalent of winning the lottery: the odds are virtually nonexistent, but wouldn't it be amazing. This abandonment to Goddess Fortuna masks the extent to which the monarchy infantilises the public and squats like a fat toad atop the still-existent hierarchy of class in British society."

That's a heavy burden to place on the shoulders of two young people setting off on a new life together. The fact that they managed their wedding with such aplomb, simplicity, and directness within an historical tradition of liturgical pageantry is also our own confirmation that continuity and decency still have a role to play in our national life. The small bouquet that Catherine carried up the aisle of Westminster Abbey and that eventually, after her marriage, was laid on the grave of the Unknown Warrior, was in part made up of sweet william and myrtle. Historically, these flowers have been associated with gallantry and loyalty. And so are they now.

And because they did all this so well — so perfectly! — they have created extraordinary expectations in all the places where they will one day sit upon their metaphorical thrones. In Canada's long and shy affair with the Crown, the Bagehot dictum of "a princely marriage being the brilliant edition of a universal fact" worked like a charm and renewed the franchise in many of our hearts. You could take a glimpse into the future — just a glimpse, I admit — and see something different than a Canada dwindling into just another boring republican entity. You could see a country — just like William and Catherine — magically in touch with its history.

ONE OF THE gifts that Prime Minister Stephen
Harper gave the royal couple during their first tour
in July 2011 was a souvenir 1939 edition of *Maclean's*
magazine that focused entirely on the ecstatic crowds
that came out during the cross-Canada tour of King
George VI and Queen Elizabeth, the first such trip
of a reigning monarch. It was the trip about which,
forever afterwards in her life, Queen Elizabeth, the
Queen Mother, would say: "Canada made us." That
was the exact quote evoked by her great-grandson
Prince William at the end of his triumphant trip with
his new wife, the first out of Britain after their magi-
cal wedding.

Nearly seventy-five years later, writing in the same
Maclean's magazine, I could scarcely believe what I was
able to report. Amongst the unbelievers of the Crown
in Canada, I wrote, you could almost touch the dumb-
founded chagrin, from sea to sea, at the extraordinary
success of the tour. William and Catherine didn't just
come and see and conquer: they vamped us. They did
it with warmth and charm and youthful sexiness, and
then topped it all with an historic and undeniable re-
minder that the ties that bound us "from days of yore"
still have the power to reach out and renew something
very important in our history.

As Stephen Harper — the single biggest political beneficiary of the success of the royal tour — told the two at the farewell dinner in Calgary, "You have taught a new generation of Canadians the value of our constitutional monarchy." So now "Will and Kate" are part of the Canadian story. A big part. Those monarchists like myself who have tried over the years, like Queen Elizabeth herself, not to be "fair-weather friends," were almost as stunned as the unbelievers as we watched this beautiful and caring young couple walk into our tale and hearts with such aplomb and grace to start a whole new chapter.

It was more than just a gesture that, on Canada Day, Catherine wore the maple leaf–shaped diamond pin the Queen wears so often when she comes to Canada[14] and which had been loaned to her for this trip. The maple leaf pin was also a kind of talisman of the past joining them to the future. When Catherine returns it to Her Majesty, she will be able to replace it with her new diamond pin shaped like a polar bear, the official gift from the Northwest Territories, given to the duchess in Yellowknife. It looks splendid enough for the Queen herself to borrow someday when she goes North of 60,

---

[14] Or when Canadians visit Buckingham Palace, or indeed on any sort of Canadian occasion abroad (the visit to Canada's Vimy Memorial in France, for example) or the Canadian High Commission in London.

and Her Majesty may well be North of 90 (years old) by then.

All these royal tours of Canada, momentous or modest, have distinctive characteristics. When Charles and Diana were here in 1991, for example, it was already becoming clear to observers who had close proximity to them that marital trouble was looming. Charles clearly resented the media frenzy around his wife. William, on the other hand, clearly basks in the adoration his bride evokes. The way he constantly, if unobtrusively, checked on how she was doing was touching — and convincing.

We need, right here, to go back in time again for a moment, not to the bedrock of chieftaincy in what we now know as Canada — that belongs to the original First Nations populations, and their unique tale has its own resonance with the Crown that has to be seriously considered and attended to — but to the roots of our own and current monarchical compromise. There was once another Prince William who came to be the "King of Canada," although in those days, when the British Empire was one metaphorically contiguous whole, no one in Canada would have called him that. He was just the King. He was also the first monarch to set foot in the country — not when he was King, of course, but when he was a rising young officer in the Royal Navy. William was the third son of the reigning sovereign, King George III, and was in command of HMS *Pegasus* in 1786 when he made his first foray to the remaining North American colonies.

It was not an auspicious first impression. William IV, as he was to become, wrote his father that "the face of this country is truly deplorable. The seasons as far backward as the beginning of April: a small brushwood for the first five hundred yards in shore and then a most dreadful, inhospitable, and barren country intersected by fresh water ponds, lakes and bogs . . ."

Most Canadians reading this bleak description pretty quickly realize he made landfall just off Newfoundland, so William's first vision and views of the sainted island are not unlike those of some snobby mainland Canadians when they first go there and look down their noses at the great blasted rock of the North Atlantic's definitive fastness, the oldest and perhaps the noblest and bravest of all of Britain's former colonies and — ironically, considering the sour first impressions of that earlier William — one of the most loyal to the Royal Family.

Travelling farther into the continent, however, William started succumbing to the wonders of the land: "As for the Province of Canada [as Quebec was then known], it vastly surpasses all the accounts I can give Your Majesty of its magnitude, beauty, and fertility: the province in extent is larger than all Europe: the views in summer are magnificent, and where in England the eye commands a view of ten miles, in Canada for many leagues the corn and the sky appear to meet."

William was also the first member of the Royal Family to establish that special relationship with the First Nations population that continues to this day, mystifies republicans (who consider the historic relationship specious and condescending), and often baffles and sometimes embarrasses Canadian governments. Writing again to King George III, William commented on the wonderful reception he had from First Nations communities in the Cornwall area, not far from Montreal, where he was headquartered. He wrote to his father in 1787, "The Indians begin to inhabit a few miles out . . . The sensations they expressed at my visit were too strong not to be natural; their language was peculiarly pointed in saying they then saw one in whose veins flowed the same blood as in the body of their Great Father in the East, meaning Your Majesty; The Indians not only love Your Majesty but they go further in adoring, their respect being so wonderfully great for everything that relates to Your Majesty."

Put the hyperbole to "Dear Papa" to one side and you can see here some of the roots of a relationship between the Royal Family and the First Nations communities of the Canadas that grew throughout the two ensuing centuries, grew despite the consistent and debilitating marginalization of their communities and the ceaseless encroachments upon their ancient homelands, grew to the point that when today's Prince William came with his new bride to Canada in the summer of 2011, it was considered crucial that he and she take part in several First Nations–inspired events.[15]

But you do have to go all the way back to that royal tour of 1939 to find the real parallel (the trip taken by the then Princess Elizabeth and Prince Philip in 1951 was

---

[15] Actually, there is an interesting and much older aboriginal connection, in this case to Queen Anne. In 1710, a group of Mohawk chiefs from upper New York travelled to England and were presented to Anne and talked of their conversion to Christianity. In response, the Sovereign arranged for the construction of a chapel at Fort Hunter in the colony of New York's Mohawk Valley and gave them a silver communion service. Sixty-five years later, at the start of the American Revolution, the Mohawks buried their silver and sided with the British in the ensuing battles. Their reward was the confiscation of their ancestral lands by the new American government, and at the invitation of the governor of Upper Canada after an intervention by the Indian leader Joseph Brant and other Six Nations representatives, the Mohawks moved to the shores of Lake Ontario just west of what is now Deseronto. They reclaimed their silver and built themselves the first of several churches, each of which featured an altarpiece containing the Creed, the Lord's Prayer and the Ten Commandments, along with the Royal Arms and a bell, all donated by King George III. Today, Christ Church in Tyendinaga Mohawk Territory is recognized as a National Historic Site, but long before that designation, it had been made a Chapel Royal by the Sovereign.

also a huge success, but there wasn't nearly so much at stake as there was in 1939 and 2011). In 1939, George and Elizabeth actually had to prove themselves worthy of being King and Queen of Canada; in 2011, by contrast, Canada had to show it wanted to retain — and was worthy of retaining — a constitutional monarchy.

THE JOURNEY THROUGH the twentieth century to the beginning of the twenty-first, and that wedding of the other William and his Kate, has clearly not been an easy trip for many Canadians with royalist sympathies, especially for those who came of age or were born after the demise of the Age of Deference (somewhere between 1960 and 1965). I was born into a Canada that, for the most part, had no problem with the monarchy and for whom the looming Coronation of the young Queen Elizabeth was the most exciting thing to happen since the end of the Second World War. The only parallel in excitement I can recall was the advent of television, and it was parallel because the two — television and the Coronation — came together, or at least they did in our house.

The year was 1953 and I was not quite nine. My bossy older sister had just turned eleven. We were both sprawled on the carpeted floor directly facing "IT," elbows down and chins expectantly up, supported by palms. My mother was seated in one of the two armchairs of the upstairs study. This was the "Twice-Around-the-Clock-Room," as described by my decorator/journalist mother in *Canadian House and Home:* a master bedroom by night, a family study by day — a clever 1950s variant to all the subterranean "rec" rooms being carved out of dank old basements. My Scottish grandmother, my mother's mother, Granny Dickinson, was seated in the other armchair.

"IT" was the first television set in the neighbourhood and had been bought two months earlier in preparation for this very moment. The date was June 2, the day of the Coronation. We waited an age while my father was on his knees fiddling with the dials. Finally he got the vertical and horizontal holds straightened out. Many neighbours were there with us. Since our purchase, two or three other neighbours had also bought sets for the same reason, and it was accepted that we all had to share with those who had remained skeptical of this new consumer contraption but nevertheless still wanted to see the Coronation.

In my Grade Two class at Oriole Park Public School, we had each just been given a large copper coronation coin with a profile of the Queen on one side and the royal cipher — EIIR — on the other. I have it still, and up to then I don't think I had ever received anything quite so precious. I saw it as somehow coming mysteriously and directly from Buckingham Palace. My granny and I knew all the details of the Coronation. We knew that the British Broadcasting Corporation was going to film the service and jet planes of the Royal Canadian Air Force, each outfitted with a special darkroom to develop the film en route, would fly each reel to Canada as it was received, to be aired on the Canadian Broadcasting Corporation shortly after the airplanes landed. Amazingly, we would be watching the Coronation in Canada on the same day it happened in London: an historic first, and John Fraser and his Scottish granny were on top of this story from start to finish.

Granny Dickinson had even bought me a special lead Coronation coach set for Christmas, and I was constantly trotting the poor Queen and Prince Philip and a select number of the Queen's horses and Queen's men down the Mall. As I could lift the roof of the golden state coach, I often felt the need to make sure the Queen was still sitting properly with her hand in a permanent semi-wave, a wave directed to all her people, which included my granny and me, of course, but also to those handsome Zulu warriors and their bare-chested wives as seen in the pages of *National Geographic* magazine, not to mention the colourful Sikhs of India, the busy Chinese of Hong Kong, the dour Boers from South Africa, the beautiful Maori from New Zealand, the well-tanned Australians in their bizarre swimsuits and bathing caps, the warmly clad Inuit from the Northwest Territories of Canada, and — my idol — Harry Belafonte, all by himself, from Jamaica.

She was ours and we were all hers. There wasn't a jewel in the Imperial State Crown whose history and dimensions we didn't know. Granny D and I knew the weight of the big golden orb and the small golden orb, the length of the jewelled sceptre, and the engraving pattern along the blade of the Sword of State. We knew how many little ermine it took to form the border on her coronation train, and how far below the knees the buttons on the silk breeches of the pageboys were fastened. No one was more immersed in this royal porn than we were.

We also knew that during two very holy moments in the service — when the Archbishop of Canterbury anointed her head and *naked breast* with holy oil, and later when she took Holy Communion (the wine for which came from grapes grown in a vineyard near

Bethlehem, while the sacred water, following purifica-
tion, was from the River Jordan) — the television cameras would be turned away. Our eyes would be averted
at both these very private moments. I was *so* relieved.
Ever since I had read an account of the forthcoming service in the *Illustrated London News* and learned that the
archbishop, Dr. Geoffrey Fisher, was going to make the
sign of the cross with the holy oil on her *naked breast*, I
became concerned about the Queen's right to privacy. I
think that at the time I thought it would be okay if I had
a glimpse of the naked breast. I would respect the privacy and be proud of the viewing privilege. But I wasn't
so sure about the rest of the world. Actually, I was pretty
sure the rest of the world shouldn't be allowed to see this.
I was also unaware at the time that (a) it was only at the
very top of the breast — the collarbone almost — that
the sign of the cross was made, so there was nothing
untoward at all about the business, and (b) according to
her famous nanny, Miss Marion Crawford ("Crawfie"),
the only total privacy Queen Elizabeth has ever enjoyed
was during the nine months she was lodged inside her
mother's womb, so she had clearly dealt with the privacy
issue years before.[16]

---

[16]   Also, years later, I read Roald Dahl's wonderful memoir of his
childhood, *Boy,* and discovered that he went to a private school in England

It was a black-and-white coronation on television, of course. It would be two days before the movie houses had the colour version. We all went to that too, standing up for the royal anthem before the film had even started, as we did for every matinee film I ever went to in my childhood. This time, though, it seemed weird to be singing "God Save the Queen" instead of "God Save the King." Exciting, I guess, in the way that all change is exciting, but also weird.

But what precisely ensued in Canada after the Coronation to transform the euphoria for the young Queen into the seemingly prevailing indifference for the aging Queen is not entirely clear in my own mind. Professional historians would no doubt point to the Quiet Revolution in Quebec; the full consequences of postwar immigration; growing Canadian nationalism, which reached some sort of apotheosis with the centennial of Confederation and Expo 67; the Vietnam War; and the "student revolution" of the late 1960s as part and parcel not only of the decline in deference but also the decline in identification with the symbols that had once bound

---

where the headmaster, the self-same Dr. Fisher before he became such a high and mighty prelate of the church, got his jollies by savagely caning little boys. That tweaked my old concern about the Queen's being so exposed to his gaze, until I realized baser things turned him on and I needn't have worried so much.

the country together, the "British monarchy" being the
most obvious. Canadian passports used to describe all
Canadian citizens as "British subjects" — this was meant
to give Canadians respect in countries where Great Britain carried far more clout than Canada. The decline of
British influence soon enough made this safety clause
irrelevant, and with it came the emerging idea that we
had a "foreign" head of state.

In the excitement of the 1967 Centennial celebrations — "the last good year" in Canada, if you
follow Pierre Berton's accounting of the country's for-
tunes — and the early years of the prime ministership
of that other Pierre, the idea that we had "grown up" and
had no need of our former colonial master really took
hold. The fact that few people in Canada had regarded
Britain as a "colonial master" was almost beside the
point. The subsequent Trudeau initiative to patriate the
remaining small clauses of the Constitution seemed to
typify the mood.

A friend of mine who worked in the British Foreign
Office at the time said to me one day, with that ironic
and occasionally insufferable English condescension
that fuels antipathy: "Well, it looks as if we are going
to let you people actually have a revolution." I wanted
to reach out and turn his nose as he talked, but I knew

what he was getting at: no one in Britain, least of all the Sovereign, and least of all anyone in the British government, was trying to prevent Canada from being Canada in whatever way the country wanted to be. What it seemed we wanted during the patriation process was a sense that we had finally "arrived" and were "on our own."

The only trouble was that imbedded in our own way of doing things was the notion of the Crown, with a Sovereign who was now officially the "Queen of Canada" sitting on a throne — an actual throne that resided in Westminster Abbey, and a metaphorical throne that was lodged in the Canadian Senate and throughout ten legislatures in ten Canadian provinces. And what on earth should we do about *that*? What on earth would we do with *her*? What on earth were we to do with the fractious, bilingual, and bicultural country that soon enough would be multicultural — with a vengeance?

In time, Pierre Trudeau made his deals. Because the issue of the monarchy seemed still so contentious with the provincial governments, he would leave it to one side, or rather he considered it not important enough to wreck the entire process. But then there was the problem of Quebec, and the problem of Quebec wasn't exactly the problem of the Crown, and here we come to probably the single most salient and interesting misunderstood reality about the Crown in Canada: its role in Quebec.

To start with, Quebec has lived under a monarchy since 1534. Quick, now! Name the first King of Canada. Of course you can't, even if you are from Quebec. The province which emblazons *"Je me souviens"* on its official crest and all its licence plates remembers only selectively. Often it only remembers hurt and defeat, leavened with a fair dose of defiance, all of which admittedly works as a kind of glue, but it's a spongy sort of glue that doesn't hold together all that well all the time, and it leaves no room for the useful shards of history. So the name of the first King of Canada — never known as such, but that is what he was — is *le roi* François I.[17] To quote the official brochure issued by the Senate of Canada, he "was the first King to encourage explorers to lead expeditions to the New World. In 1533, he signed a treaty with Spain and Portugal that gave France the right to navigate in all unmapped territories." François also personally financed

[17] If you like memory games, here are the names of the other kings of Canada who ruled from France until 1763, when the kingship of Canada passed by treaty from France to Britain after the Battle of the Plains of Abraham: François I, Henri III, Henri IV, Louis XIII, Louis XIV, Louis XV. Here's a memory-jogging clue: *François × 1, Henri × 2, and Louis × 3.* Go ahead: impress your friends. Ask them if they can name the first six monarchs who ruled over Canada.

Jacques Cartier's famous trip from Saint-Malo to the Gaspé. Let it be noted, because much of the subsequent history has been so fraught, that Cartier was welcomed by the First Nations population, who hadn't a real clue that their historic territories were about to be proclaimed for Cartier's King, but nevertheless came to the rescue of the explorer's crew when its numbers were decimated during the first winter: the first "hint" of the challenge facing every outsider who was to come to Canada.

For over two centuries, French rule in Canada continued — rough and ready — until the expansionist ambitions of the British colonies to the south and quarrels in Europe brought an English–French war on two continents and ended forever the rule of French kings in North America. With that end came the beginning of Canada's perpetual challenge of dealing with what Lord Durham would later call the struggle of two nations within the bosom of a single state.

Abandoned by France after the Conquest, the strongest unifying institution left to Quebeckers was their (Roman Catholic) Church, and the sense of identity with *église et patrie* became, in short order, ferocious. Eventually, and helped enormously by the repugnance felt by the Roman Catholic Church for the sense of destiny engendered by a mostly Protestant United

States of America, followed smartly by the excesses of terror and anti-clericism of the French Revolution, Quebec — through its church and political leaders — came to see the Crown as a protector of language and religious rights, as indeed it was.

That's why the arrival of King George VI and Queen Elizabeth in Quebec City at the start of their 1939 tour was such a success and why they were beloved figures in Quebec and why their pictures were in many Québecois kitchens alongside the Pope's, and why prayers for their health and long lives were said at many masses.

These things happened and were felt strongly, although since 1964 they have become mostly obliterated in the newer mantra. The year is significant since it is at the heart of the Quiet Revolution, which commenced a few years earlier as Quebeckers threw off old mantles and donned a different suit. That was also the year of "Truncheon Saturday" in Quebec City, a memorable juncture in the clashes between Anglophone and Francophone Canada, with the poor Queen caught in the middle through no fault of her own.

The actual incident was less impressive than its immediate and lasting effect. During the 1964 royal tour of Canada, the Queen and Prince Philip were scheduled to visit the Quebec Legislature. There had been rumblings of trouble, but Prime Minister Lester Pearson assured the Queen these would not amount to anything much. In the end, independence-minded Quebeckers lined the roadway to the legislature but turned their backs on the royal cavalcade as it passed by, caught by news photographers and beamed to front pages around the world. Elsewhere, over-eager or inexperienced (or both) police charged a peaceful crowd of monarchists and anti-monarchists, beating them up and arresting people indiscriminately. The incident, one of the seminal moments in Quebec's Quiet Revolution, is clearly a major event in the reign of the Queen and figures prominently in Ben Pimlott's definitive biography of Elizabeth[18] where Prime Minister Pearson emerges in less than heroic colours:

"Anticipating trouble which they had earlier predicted would not take place," Pimlott wrote, "the Canadian authorities over-reacted ... As a result, interest in the tour focused on the controversy over the security measures, and the nationalists seemed vindicated ... The public reaction in Quebec, and the lack of it elsewhere, led Pearson — who had initiated the visit in the first

---

[18]   *The Queen: A Biography of Elizabeth II* by Ben Pimlott, HarperCollins Publishers, 1996.

place[19] — to warn the Queen that the Monarchy's days in the dominion were numbered."

Here then was the seed that grew into a mantra for the next half-century. Because a few hundred protestors caused an overreaction by the Quebec police, the Liberal administration assumed the monarchy was in its waning days. The problem was that constitutionally the Crown was entrenched in the Canadian way of doing things and there were far too many Canadians who revered both the institution and the person of the Queen to go about dismantling it openly.

The solution for the political establishment, so far as I can figure it out, was to begin the process of gradual attrition: remove symbols of the Crown, lessen royal tours, upgrade the office of the governor general, change names like "Dominion of Canada." Many of these changes met with general Canadian approval, especially in the wake of the centennial year and Expo 67, when it seemed somehow right and fitting that Canadians should celebrate Canadian-ness. A compellingly honest and non-surreptitious republican argument — often espoused by Professor Michael Bliss — was that the

---

[19] To commemorate the centenary of the Charlottetown Conference of 1864, which began the formal negotiations towards Confederation in 1867.

"majesty of Canada itself" needed no royal embellish-
ments from abroad. That too was part of the rhetoric:
diminish the historic links to the Crown and embellish
the foreignness of it all — why should a foreign monarch be Canada's head of state?

When "Truncheon Saturday" drifted into the legends
of the land, it did so with a new mantra as the political
establishment, for the most part, lost heart for the very
idea of the Canadian monarchy. It did not take many
years before republican sentiment, ever polite, argued
that once the Queen died, it would be time to put our
house in order. With quiet encouragement from newly
minted institutions like the Department of Canadian
Heritage (carved out of the old Secretary of State's office
in 1993) and the office of the governor general itself, the
Crown drifted from awkward relic into a kind of shroud-
ed Ruritanian anachronism.

It all reached a kind of apogee with the governor gen-
eralship of Adrienne Clarkson, one of only two or three
truly great viceregal appointments in our past half-
century.[20] Somehow, although her closest friends and
admirers knew that she regarded herself as Canada's de

---

20   I would include Vincent Massey, the first Canadian-born governor
general and his successor, General Georges Vanier. In fact, Vanier and
Madam Clarkson are really the only two outstanding GGs; I include Mr.
Massey out of loyalty to the founder of my college.

facto head of state, Madam Clarkson managed a delicate balancing act, and only rarely did the public know how strongly she felt. Once was when she blatantly upstaged the Queen in France in 2004, during the proceedings for the sixtieth anniversary of the landings on Juno Beach. It was at this ceremony that it became most evident that Madam Clarkson saw the role of the governor general as the appropriate representative of "the Crown," and thus it was that the Queen of Canada was relegated to third position behind the Canadian "head of state" — Madam Clarkson — and her husband, John Ralston Saul.

In looking back on "Truncheon Saturday," I wonder if the ghost of Lester B. Pearson was haunting the precincts in Lévis in the summer of 2011, when Prince William and his duchess did their walkabout to adoring crowds of Quebeckers. In fact, on the eve of the Duke and Duchess of Cambridge's first royal tour of Canada, a curious article appeared in the *Globe and Mail* about a young Francophone, who against all odds (or at least the odds of the *Globe's* reporter) saw more than token purpose in the constitutional monarchy of Canada and Quebec. Of the dozens of separatists who got onto page one of the nation's newspapers, who were featured on CBC and CNN and the BBC, I would like to give you one young man, named Monsieur Étienne Boisvert, who

THE SECRET OF THE CROWN

adorned an inside page under the banner heading "Dieu protège la reine, says young Quebecker":

"He speaks French first, yet pledges unabashed allegiance to an English Queen," began the reporter. "He's 22 years old but far more interested in constitutional monarchy than the celebrity appeal of Will and Kate. His name is Étienne Boisvert, and he is the rarest of Quebec species — *le monarchiste*. He speaks of the monarchy with pride, eloquence and conviction. In French." The article went on to say that in Quebec the majority of the Francophone population regard the monarchy and the Royal Family with indifference, but somehow this one young man seems to have come up with a rationale that defies logic. To prove the illogic, the article concludes this way:

"Mr. Boisvert says the monarchy has managed to change with the times, starting with the Magna Carta 800 years ago up to recent years when Prince Charles admitted a 'curious' institution like the monarchy can only survive if it listens to the people. Mr. Boisvert rattles off the entire quote by heart, one of his few full sentences in English in the interview.[21] 'That statement is

---

21   "Something as curious as the monarchy won't survive unless you take account of people's attitudes. After all, if people don't want it, they won't have it."

the foundation to me. The monarchy has survived 1,000 years because it adapts to the will of the people. If you and I sat down to invent a system of government, this probably wouldn't be it. But I can't think of a better one.'"

The Quiet Revolution took all of Canada down an uncertain pathway, but part of the strength of the country is that it has survived all the ensuing ups and downs and has also learned — for the most part — to leave well enough alone, constitutionally. "Well enough alone" has not stopped Canada from being the most desired destination of most immigrants in the world today. It has not stopped Canada from being the most successful multi-ethnic and multicultural country in the world. It has not stopped Canada from enjoying the benefits of its vast natural resources. It has not stopped Quebec from fiercely defending its language and cultural distinctions within a loose federation. My God, it has even managed to turn Newfoundland into a "have" province and — to the immense satisfaction of many — Ontario into a "have not." Somehow, all this has been done with a constitutional monarchy chugging away, with the Queen as a head of state, and with ever-evolving roles for the governor general and lieutenant governors acting as regents for the Crown.

It may be a strange system, but it's ours and it works.

CHAPTER TWO

Tribal Monarchy and Local Royalty

During the First World War, the redoubtable Queen Mary was forever in and out of hospitals — sometimes three or four in an afternoon — visiting the wounded. It was on one of these tours that another and much younger family member being dragged around in her wake complained, "I'm tired and I hate hospitals." The queen's reported response encapsulated the attitude of modern monarchy. "You are a member of the Royal Family. We are NEVER tired and we LOVE hospitals!"

— From *On Royalty,* by Jeremy Paxman

M Y FIRST RENDEZVOUS WITH A CANADIAN GOV-
ernor general was early on in my teenage years.
Despite the passage of over half a century, it is steel-
bolted into my brain. The setting was Upper Canada
College, the all-boys private school in midtown Toronto,
during the early 1960s, when the reconstruction of the
main Upper School building had been completed. A little bijou of a chapel, seating thirty or forty endangered
souls, was the last item on the building list. It was the
gift of the Right Honourable Vincent Massey, C.H.,[22] the
first Canadian-born governor general, and he had only

---

22   C.H. stands for "Companion of Honour" — one of the highest honours the Queen can personally bestow on one of her subjects. It is also an
honour which Canadians can accept. One of the most recent in Canada
is former prime minister Jean Chrétien, as staunch a monarchist as any
royalist would want — when it suits his purposes. Another is Professor
Anthony Pawson, the extraordinary University of Toronto researcher
into the genetic formulations of cancer. Both Mr. Massey's C.H. medal
and Professor Pawson's are proudly lodged at Massey College.

recently stepped down to be succeeded by the noblest of them all, General Georges Vanier, the first Francophone governor general. The chapel had been carved out of the old bicycle shed adjacent to the College's quadrangle. It was there, throughout much of the construction period, that a small but determined crew of fifteen-year-old smokers gathered every lunch hour in the perfect place to indulge our noxious but delightfully insidious habit. Cigarette packages had no warnings on them in those days. Instead, they had alluring metaphysical flashing neon signs saying: "Smoke me" or "I am cool" or even (despite blazer with school crest, tie, white shirt, and flannel pants with cuffs) "I am a rebel."

The chapel had basically been finished for several weeks, but a couple of workmen were in there daily doing fine detailing. They both smoked, so the heavy smell of dead tobacco and cigarette ash hung usefully about the place. The workmen always vacated the premises midday to take an hour off for lunch, so it was more than perfect — it was safe. Just in case, though, guards would be placed in front of both its doors: one was from an interior stairwell in the new college building, and the other was behind the altar and a small sacristy that led directly into the quadrangle. The windows of the chapel itself were made of heavily frosted glass, so no one could tell what we were doing, although there were usually well over a hundred boys and masters immediately on the other side. If trouble looked like it was about to descend upon us, a smart rapping on whichever was the danger door would send us all rushing out the other.

The day after the chapel furniture arrived, including the altar, we knew the jig was up, and on that sunny autumn day we went there for the last time. The atmosphere seemed decidedly poignant, even to teenaged boys, who are not known for their ability to appreciate poignancy. Maybe it was just regret. Whatever: we knew our smoking hidey-hole was now "*interdit*" and it wasn't because of our respect for the Deity. The place was just getting too damn dangerous.

And then the unthinkable — if inevitable — happened. The guards on both doors banged simultaneously. Guard No. 1 came running into the chapel and blurted: "Sowby and some old guy." Sowby was Dr. Cedric Sowby, the Anglican priest who was principal of the college: a sour man who wouldn't have hesitated to expel us for our brave flouting of college prohibitions, or so we assumed. As we headed towards the other door, Guard No. 2, on quadrangle duty, also came running in and shouted one of the most dreaded words in the college lexicon: "SHEARER!!"

Mr. I. K. Shearer, the single most feared master at the college, a known sadist, a man with a closet full of whips and canes. Unmarried too, and, so far as we were concerned, beyond any sort of reasonable approach as a civilized human being with normal blood in his veins. The literary prototype here is Claggart in *Billy Budd* or the beadle at the paupers' orphanage in *Oliver Twist* or even Inspector Javert in *Les Misérables*. Anyway, you get the gist, and now the chapel — our beloved smoker — had come to his baleful notice. Split-second choices are never easy, especially when both options are terrifying. Rush out into the arms of Dr. Sowby with hastily stubbed butts all over his chapel floor, and we all assumed we would be out of the school and into our parents' righteous wrath before the day was done. Rush out into Shearer's arms and a pitiless, savage beating would inevitably ensue. The choice was a no-brainer. Out we all went into the stern but clearly delighted arms of the Sadist.

Well, nearly all of us. I was closest to the main entrance and thus the farthest from the sacristy doorway leading to the quadrangle. I knew I couldn't get out before Dr. Sowby came in, so I did the only sensible thing someone in my situation could possibly do. I sank to my knees and raise my closed palms heavenward. Almost simultaneously, Mr. Shearer poked his head through one door to see if any other victims were lurking, and Dr. Sowby and some "old guy" came in the entrance from the college interior. At least that's what I assumed was happening, because I heard, from behind my head, Dr. Sowby saying: "Shearer, what are you doing here?" And he said, "Sorry, sir; sorry, gentlemen. I was just checking." And out he went to deal with seven of the eight miscreants, whom he had lined up against a brick wall. I learned soon afterwards that he marched them off to his office and one by one gave them six brutal swats of his most lethal switch — the one he flexed several times in the air before bringing it crashing down on his bent-over victims' backsides. Not me, though. Back in the chapel during the ensuing and deadly calm which followed, I heard only a low mumbling behind me. I didn't budge an inch.

Then, miraculously, there was no more mumbling. The only sounds were those drifting in from the quadrangle. I assumed Dr. Sowby and the "old guy" had left, but I still didn't dare to budge. Moments later, the bell rang, signalling the end of the lunch break and time to return to classes. I cautiously looked around. There was no one fore or aft, but all the way up the aisle of the chapel were stamped-out cigarette butts which apparently Dr. Sowby hadn't noticed, or at least I prayed he hadn't.

It seemed as if the Deity was on my side for a change, and there was a real bounce in my step as I went back to my scheduled class. Over the next fifteen minutes my cohorts arrived, one by one, walking very gingerly, and the miracle seemed even more amazing.

The ringing of the classroom intercom phone ended this idyll. The master answered it and I heard him say: "Yes, he's here. I'll send him to you right away." He hung up and peered around the classroom. "Ah, there you are, Fraser. Dr. Sowby wants you to come to his office right away. Be quick about it and come back here right after."

How elation can turn into such instant dread is astonishing. If my chums came back to the classroom with a wince in each step, each of my own forward steps to Dr. Sowby's seemed weighted with lead. "Go right in, Fraser. Dr. Sowby's waiting for you," said his secretary, when I finally arrived. I walked in and there the principal was, looking rather small and beak-nosed behind his big desk.[23]

---

[23] Dr. Sowby had been my confirmation instructor two years earlier, but the experience had not brought us very close. On one occasion, the confirmation class filed out of his office and I saw that two boys were waiting to see him. I learned later that, for his convenience, he had booked them both in for a caning after our class as punishment for some sort of misdemeanour. This episode later led to my first experience of censorship. I wrote what I thought was a brilliant satire for the *College Times* of the confusion in Dr. Sowby's confirmation class about a strict understanding

"Ah, Fwaser," he said, in his distinctive crackly voice, complete with a slushy *r* and wobbly *l*. "I just wanted you to know how pweased His Excellency was to see a boy at pwayer. Very gwatifying."

I stood like a dumb ox before his desk, not quite taking it in.

"Who, sir?" I asked.

"Mr. Massey. He came to see All Souls' Chapel today. We were at the back of the chapel when you were pwaying. Thank you, Fwaser. That's all for now. I just wanted to let you know. You can weturn to your class now."

I was fifteen when this happened and when I first gave thanks to God for creating Vincent Massey.

A year after the chapel incident, I left Upper Canada College under something of a cloud. It was the same year Conrad Black, my friend and colleague of so many years, also left UCC under his very own cloud: I left of my own volition for flunking exams and he was expelled for stealing them.[24] I came back to the school the

---

of the Bible's admonition to "turn the other cheek." The student editor refused to even discuss why it was rejected. *Editors! What can you do about them?*

24   My moral purity during this difficult personal period couldn't have been higher, however, because I got the grand mark of seven out of one hundred in physics. Clearly I had bought no exams. When my perplexed father, who had never seen a single-digit mark on a report card before,

following autumn to pick up a prize for the one thing I was good at during those days: public speaking. It was handed to me on Prize Day by Governor General Vanier. The book was Rudyard Kipling's *Stalky & Co.*, and as General Vanier handed it to me, he looked down at the title and then up into my face.

"Well," he said, almost whispering as I gazed somewhat stupefied into that amazingly avuncular, sad face, "I think you're a bit old for this, but the binding is beautiful. Congratulations."

THAT WAS THE first time I saw the Vaniers, and it was through a haze of teenage defiance. I remember his extraordinary face and the aura of reserve and dignity, and I think I remember her gazing on sweetly, but that may be one of those fanciful *post facto* memories. That's because, in time, Pauline Vanier became one of the most important people in my life, and today whenever I think of her, I feel enveloped in uncritical affection and bask in all the remembered warmth and spiritual generosity. The day she died in Compiègne in 1991, at the great

asked how on earth it came about, I was equally perplexed: "I don't know, Dad. I didn't even write the exam." But then he was dealing with my poor mentally disordered mother and I had found it safer simply to block out the real world, including anything as peripheral as exams and UCC.

age of ninety-two, is forever etched in my consciousness because it was the same day that Mr. Shen Zhong-
hua slammed his dilapidated bicycle into a delivery van
at the foot of a hill on Christie Street in Toronto. The
proximity of events is relevant to this tale, so bear with
me here. It is difficult to describe how symbolic figures and real people interact, or how "heritage" works
to everyday advantage, but for me the death of this mi-
raculous old lady and the technically unrelated accident
of a Chinese political refugee make the point, at least to
my satisfaction.

The two events are hitched in my mind because, sec-
onds after I had hung up on the long-distance call from
Madame Vanier's son, Jean Vanier, in France, my sister
called to say Mr. Shen was in hospital getting a broken
leg put in a cast. He had been charged with reckless
driving, she added, and the van owner was demanding
exorbitant damages.

Grieve for the dead, worry about the living: life sometimes happens in bizarre clumps. Mammy, as Pauline
Vanier was called by everyone who was close to her in
her last two or three decades, lived a life as full as anyone's in the old Canada. After General Vanier died, she
retired to the small village in France outside Compiègne
to live out her last years at the mother house of the

international L'Arche movement for mentally handi-
capped adults, founded by her son. Her final illness last-
ed less than a week, and then her mighty spirit fled her
body.

Mr. Shen, on the other hand, was only thirty-eight at
the time and had been born into a poor Chinese peasant
family in rural Shanxi province, the fourth of six children and the only one in the entire history of his family
to get a higher education. An agronomist, he was on an
exchange visit to Canada at the time of the Tiananmen
slaughter and virtually jumped into our arms when my
sister made the mistake of expressing some concern
over his plight. Since I had once worked as a journalist
in China, I bore the heavy burden of being the Chinese
expert in the family, and before long Mr. Shen and either
my sister or I were to be seen making the dogged rounds
of immigration and manpower offices in Toronto.

Mammy died surrounded by people who loved her
for herself and for all that her remarkable life represented. Her sons and daughter were nearby. A network
of people associated with the L'Arche movement around
the world held a vigil in her honour and cradled her in
their hearts on her final passage. The Queen sent a private message of concern to Jean Vanier. In Toronto, Mr.
Shen was for all practical purposes alone save for our

family, which was small comfort in the night, when he went about his work at a twenty-four-hour gas station.

The job came with illegally low wages and a boss who cheated him of a few dollars most weeks by alleging accounting inaccuracies. Since Mr. Shen never made mistakes with money, this was more than a grievance: it struck at his sense of honour and fairness. There was nothing he could do about it, though, and he always gave in because he knew — as his boss knew even better — that there were a dozen people ready to take his job at any given time.

In his spare moments, Mr. Shen held down another (part-time) job, gave volunteer tai chi chuan instruction at a neighbourhood YMCA, and attended an ever-increasing variety of self-help courses. He lived in a closet of a room in a boarding house a few blocks from where he had the accident, bought six-month supplies of staple foods at emporiums I never knew existed, clothed himself at Goodwill, and never failed to listen to *The World at Six* on CBC Radio after he awoke from the four to five hours of sleep he allowed himself six days out of seven. On Sundays, he did his intensive studying and his laundry. He wrote letters to his wife and two children in China, sometimes visited us, and — wherever else he went — rigorously made a point of avoiding Chinatown (for reasons that seem obvious to defecting Chinese and overwrought to middle-class native Canadians).

The bicycle accident was a catastrophe, a far bigger one than most of us could even begin to comprehend. He was returning from the gas-station job. The half-hour ride got him home around 7:30 a.m., and the leisurely free-wheel down the final hill was one of the few enjoyable moments. Until, that is, this particular morning, when he applied the brakes and discovered he didn't have brakes anymore. He tried to slow the bike by skidding along the sidewalk curb and dragging a foot, but everything was happening too fast and the next thing he knew he had crashed into the parked van and was splayed on the sidewalk in agony, his right leg twisted at a queer angle.

The owner of the van never once helped him, but instead shouted obscenities along with what Mr. Shen described as "unfriendly" observations on the Chinese as a race. Within minutes, presumably prompted by a telephone call from the van owner, two — *two!* — squad cars were on the scene and four officers. An officer in the first car talked to the van owner, then demanded some ID from Mr. Shen, and finally charged him with reckless driving. Another officer in another squad car, who had already helped him up, drove him to a hospital. The crumpled bicycle was abandoned and presumably ended up in the garbage; it was certainly not returned to Mr. Shen.

The nice cop said that the nasty cop's rap could probably be beaten, but at this point Mr. Shen wasn't taking too much in. He was wondering how he could hold on to two jobs, how he could avoid disappointing the senior citizens at his tai chi sessions, how he was going to get to his own classes. He thought of Chairman Mao's favourite fable, of the old man who moved a mountain, a parable from Cultural Revolution theology meant to spur the masses to impossible tasks, but then ruefully remembered that the old man had two working legs when he moved earth and stone.

A week after she died, Mammy's body was flown back to Canada for a state funeral in Quebec City. It may be a cliché to say that funerals are for the living, but clichés, too, are for the living. My wife, Elizabeth, and I needed an occasion fixed on some proximity to her to focus the awful sense of loss. Our friendship had been one of the few pure perquisites of a life in journalism. On the way to a posting in Beijing nearly fifteen years earlier, I had badgered my way into her life on the excuse of an interview. She refused me twice, but Elizabeth and I just turned up at her door anyway. She let us step over the threshold. Not a year passed after the China post-ing that we didn't spend time together, in either Canada or France. The telephone bills were ridiculous. She has held each of my daughters in her arms, and the force of her crunching bear hugs is implanted deep in whatever understanding I have of what it means to be truly alive and truly connected. *Nothing* was going to keep us away from Quebec City, so my sister volunteered to look after the children. And Mr. Shen.

The Queen sent a wreath. The governor general came. Soldiers of her beloved regiment, the Royal 22nd, ushered people to their seats in the cathedral, bore her body through the nave, and carried it to the vault hol-lowed out of the rock of the Citadel, where she was placed beside General Vanier. At the service, Jean Vanier said that his mother was no different at the end than she had been throughout the lifetime he had known her. She was a little girl, he said, longing to be loved. That was true enough, but I also remembered when she was in St. John's, Newfoundland, in 1966, and let loose a flash of Franco-Irish ire at a tree-planting ceremony in Bowring Park. It was less than a year before her husband was to die in office, and a civic official, self-important but no doubt well enough intentioned, roughly and noisily barred a stray ragamuffin from getting a closer look at the viceregal couple. Eyes flashing with anger, Mammy left her husband and barged past the official to get to the child. She jackknifed her large frame to bring herself to his level and, in the subsequent brief encounter — just a gesture to be sure, but nevertheless a gesture — she transformed the circle of onlookers into penitents in the cause of simple decency.

After the burial, the regimental band of the Van Doos played "God Save the Queen" and "O Canada," and the regiment marched past the crypt. It seemed that in burying Mammy Vanier we were sealing up a notion of Canada in the cold stone high above the St. Lawrence River. The notion is hard to express without sounding maudlin, but you could point to the old lady and say, "She was it." I never expected to encounter it again.

Mr. Shen's court day was twice postponed. He turned up alone both times at the courthouse in the old city hall in Toronto and was sent away both times. The van owner and the constables — the "witnesses" — never seemed to be there, and inquiries by Mr. Shen simply led to a new date. The business left him confused but unbowed. It was while he was preparing for his third date that he finally told my sister what was going on. She phoned me and the two of us called an emergency meeting with him.

We told Mr. Shen that he must have a lawyer. He wouldn't hear of it. He had already somehow insinuated himself into the library of Osgoode Hall Law School and read everything connected to reckless-driving charges. Lawyers, he announced, were too expensive. I had learned by this time not to proffer money, as either gift or loan. He was extremely proud of his independence, and the few dollars he had been forced to accept from me when he first made his penniless decision to remain in Canada had been returned within three months — with interest (calculated at prevailing rates, which he had checked out with two banks and one trust company).

He also confided to my sister and me that if he didn't have to go to prison he would be bringing out his wife and children under the Canada–China family reunification programme. After trying to reassure him there was no possibility of his going to prison, we also tried to disengage him from the wildly premature scheme of bringing his family to Canada. While Mr. Shen had shown ingenuity in holding on to both his jobs since the accident, despite crutches for several weeks and with even less sleep, he was clearly not sufficiently well set up to cope with the considerable extra burden of a family. My sister and I knew a lot about these sorts of things.

"I think it's all right," said Mr. Shen quietly. "I've saved fifteen —"

"For heaven's sake, Shen," I said to him. "Do you have any idea what it will cost just to fly them here? Fifteen hundred dollars might bring one of them."

"Not fifteen hundred," he said, still quietly. "Fifteen thousand."

"Fifteen thousand!" we exclaimed. "That's one, five, zero, zero, zero. Three zeroes."

"Yes," he said, and he smiled this time. "One, five, zero, zero, zero. I've saved it. I think it's enough to get started. My wife's English is not very good, so she will have to go to school for six months before she starts a job."

My sister and I stared at each other, our collective debts crashing against Mr. Shen's fiscal acuity. Together, without saying a word, we retreated from our role as advisers, though we had the grace to keep ourselves — at least for the moment — from soliciting financial advice.

The next day, Mr. Shen and I met outside the courthouse fifteen minutes before he had been told to show up. He was clutching a file containing various papers he was going to use in his defence. Everything had been copied by hand from the law books. He had gone over them with us the night before, and it was all perfectly incomprehensible. My sister and I had quietly worked it out that, if things went badly, I would try to intervene in the process and get another stay in the proceedings so we could hire a bloody lawyer. That was as close to a strategy as we could come up with.

Together Mr. Shen and I entered the courthouse and found our way, through a jungle of well-dressed lawyers and their nervous clients, to the designated courtroom. It was a woman who was presiding at the bench. We arrived just as she was pronouncing her verdict on some hapless youth up on a drunk-driving charge, and she was severe with him. She seemed in an irritable mood. Truly, the karma was not good. Mr. Shen had begun shaking quite visibly the moment we walked through the portals and, as he sat beside me, we might as well have been hooked up by electrodes, so completely had he transmitted his terror.

Shortly after three p.m., a court official called for "Mr." — (long pause) — "Shunga-gunga-whee" and told him to approach the bench. The judge looked down at me and asked Mr. Shen if I was his legal counsel. "No," I said, almost in a whisper. I was really upset. "I'm his friend. I guess I'm his sponsor."

She snorted, or at least it sounded to me like a snort.

Mr. Shen was sworn in. He looked very small before

the judge's bench. I had the impression of his slowly being engulfed by the whole setting.

"What's that you're holding?" Her Honour asked peremptorily, pointing to Mr. Shen's file of papers. "Let me see it."

The papers were taken by the court official and handed to the judge. After reading some documentation of her own, she spent an agonizing two minutes perusing Mr. Shen's file before handing it back to the official and to Mr. Shen.

"Well?" she said to the official. The tone was unmistakably brusque.

"Your Honour," he said, "the witnesses are not here."

"Of course they're not," she said. Her eyes were . . . angry. Very angry. "This gentleman has already had his case postponed twice. What an introduction to our justice system." She rearranged her papers. "You are free to go, sir."

Mr. Shen was locked into position. His head swivelled towards me but his feet couldn't turn. The court official approached him. "You can go now," he said.

I got up and went to the bar and motioned. "Come on, Shen," I hissed, "let's get out of here."

"I'm free?" Mr. Shen asked.

"You're free. It's all over."

I know I said that, because when Mr. Shen later re-
galed my sister with what had happened, he said that's
what I said. All I can really remember is trying to
fight back the tears. I had learned that old Canada had
never truly died, because in the judge's face, I had seen
Mammy's eyes.

IF VINCENT MASSEY was a great transition figure between the British pooh-bahs who acted as regents for
the Sovereign prior to his time, General Vanier was the
perfect transition to a bilingual and bicultural Canada.
These transitions came when Canadians were ready to
refashion their links with the Crown and develop further the notion of the viceregal regents both nationally
and provincially, an evolutionary process which has
gone off in a variety of directions, most of them largely unnoticed by a majority of Canadians and, on the
whole, good. General Vanier was such a palpably good
man, and for those who keep track of such things, he
set an almost impossibly high benchmark for his successors. Of course he had the experience of serving in
two world wars as part of his Identikit, but I think more
than the notion of a venerable soldier, it was his trans-
parent goodness and otherworldly spirit that impressed

Canadians about the man and my beloved Mammy. No one even remotely like them got into Rideau Hall until Adrienne Clarkson and John Ralston Saul took over the helm, and their appeal was strikingly different, though no less effective at its best. And it is the changing nature of "local royalty," expressed through the viceregal offices of governor general and the provincial lieutenant governors, that are the most tangible evidence that the Crown works well in Canada.

Since Massey's time — and he was appointed the first Canadian-born governor general in 1952, just before King George VI died — there have essentially been two models or styles for the role of national regent, which, in effect, is what a governor general is. The first we could call the "Right Royal" style, and certainly Mr. Massey, the founder of my college in the University of Toronto, was the very model of a modern "Right Royal" governor general. Indeed, many thought him more English than the English, more royal than the Royals.[25]

The highest exemplar of this model, however, was

---

[25]   In his magisterial two-volume biography of Vincent Massey, Claude Bissell reports on two Englishmen of "impeccable credentials" discussing the 1935 appointment of the anglophile Massey as Canada's new High Commissioner. "They agree he has excellent qualities," writes Bissell, "then one adds plaintively, 'But damn it all, the fellow always makes one feel like a bloody savage.'"

not Mr. Massey but the saint-like General Vanier,[26] who was governor general from 1959 to 1967, when he died in office, symbolically during Canada's centennial celebrations. He never aped anyone or any culture. His loyalty to the Sovereign, however, was unquestioned and unremitting. This model reveres the Sovereign, regardless of who sits on the throne, and carries on his or her duties in the name of the King or Queen but never forgets — or lets people forget — where the "fount of honour" rests.

The second type of Canadian regent we could call "Crown Legatee," in that the person of the Sovereign is far less important than the person representing the Crown, who — in effect — is the functioning head of state of the country. This is not just semantics, because the differences and different interpretations of the role governors general play in the country have caused real debates and occasional eruptions.

There has been no better exemplar of the "Crown Legatee" than Adrienne Clarkson, who was scrupulously respectful of the Sovereign in public but rarely hesitated to push an agenda to promote the role of the governor general of Canada as the actual (rather than de facto)

---

26   Also, I say "saint-like" for more than metaphoric embellishment. In fact, he and his wife, Pauline Vanier, are actually on the road to sainthood, having been nominated together for beatification in 1992, shortly after Madame Vanier's death the same year.

Above: Queen Victoria's Diamond Jubilee in 1897 is duly noted at the Canada Atlantic Railway office at the corner of Spark and Elgin Streets in Ottawa. **Below:** At the same time in London, capital of the Empire, the Queen Empress herself is carried through the streets in her new phaeton — the same small carriage Queen Elizabeth II uses today during the Trooping of the Colour.

When Edward, the Prince of Wales, made his first trip to Canada in 1919, he was made an honorary chief of the Stony Creek Indians (now Saik'uz First Nation) in Alberta. He clearly liked the ceremonial outfit and managed to keep his cigar going in his right hand, while showing off the family's signet ring on his left.

Prince Edward kept the headdress he received from the Stony Creek Indians and wore it again in Banff on the same 1919 trip. He was a huge hit with Canadians in all areas of the country, but his particular identification with First Nations communities and western Canada was widely noticed.

By 1923, Prince Edward had purchased the E. P. (Edward Prince) Ranch in Alberta and was revelling in the rancher's life. He sent this picture of himself, sitting on top of one of his bulls, to his father, King George V.

The Duke and Duchess of York on their wedding day, April 26, 1923. The second son of King George V was "doomed" to become king when in 1936 the abdication crisis unfolded.

Two years after King George VI and Queen Elizabeth ascended to the throne, they took an historic trip to Canada — the first by a reigning sovereign. Here, in May 1939, Prime Minister William Lyon Mackenzie King, in full court dress, greets them upon their arrival by ship in Quebec City.

The King and Queen of Canada arrive at the Parliament Buildings in Ottawa on their 1939 tour. Prime Minister William Lyon Mackenzie King, still in full court dress, welcomes the monarch and his wife.

King George VI and Queen Elizabeth take the royal salute before the Parliament Buildings in Ottawa (1939).

King George VI gives the Royal Assent to Canadian parliamentary bills from the throne chair in the Senate Chamber (1939).

The huge success of the royal tour meant that the Liberal Prime Minister W. L. M. King was never far away from photo opportunities. Here he is, finally out of his full court dress, posing with the royal couple at the Banff Springs Hotel in late May 1939. "Canada made us," the Queen would later say about their cross-country trip.

King George VI's eldest daughter and heir to the throne, Princess Elizabeth, marries her dream prince, Philip Mountbatten of Greece, on November 20, 1947.

Princess Elizabeth attends the Calgary Stampede on her first royal tour of Canada in 1951. J. B. Cross, president of the Calgary Stampede, helps Princess Elizabeth down to the Navajo rug in her "all-Canadian" mink coat, while Prince Philip waits in the coach.

Princess Elizabeth and Prince Philip proceeded westward from Calgary on their 1951 tour. At Sicamous, British Columbia, school children gather at a whistle stop to greet Princess Elizabeth before she continues on to Vancouver.

Governor General Viscount Alexander of Tunis threw a square dance party at Rideau Hall to celebrate the end of Princess Elizabeth and Prince Philip's first tour of Canada in 1951. Exactly sixty years later, in 2011, her grandson and a future king of Canada — William, Duke of Cambridge, and his duchess, Catherine — would be in the same house at the beginning of their first tour.

Crowned and enthroned on her Coronation Day, June 2, 1953, and surrounded by all the ancient pomp and pageantry her ancient "other realm"
can muster, the new Queen of Canada officially begins her new reign.

The first Canadian-born governor general, Vincent Massey, set a standard for governors general travelling north. Here he is in Frobisher Bay, Baffin Island, in March 1956. He was an enthusiastic supporter of First Nations rights and recognition.

At La Citadelle de Québec in 1964, the Queen is escorted by the first French-Canadian governor general, Georges Vanier, founding colonel of the Royal 22nd Regiment of Canada, the famous Van Doos.

Queen Elizabeth II and Prince Philip wave goodbye at the end of their 1967 centennial year visit to Canada.

head of state in the public consciousness. She pushed it like it had never been pushed before.[27] Those of us who loved the Queen and admired Madam Clarkson were often torn. Yet no one, in the whole history of Rideau Hall, ever evoked the country quite as effectively as Adrienne Clarkson. Had she remained in high office another five or ten years, I am not sure whether this book could have been conceived and written. But her successor — Michaëlle Jean — proved the dangers inherent in this model, much as a regent who too slavishly follows British royal practice would undermine the other model.

Madam Clarkson's genius was particularly strong in evoking Canada to Canadians through her words. Her tribute to Canada's Unknown Soldier, who lay in an unmarked grave until his corpse was brought to Ottawa from the killing fields of Vimy Ridge in France with full military honours, was not simply outstanding, I don't believe, in the whole history of Canada, that there is a finer piece of patriotic rhetoric. It summoned up what Canada was and is — in both official languages. It is not

[27]   This categorization is a personal theory, and debatable, but I would list the Canadian-born or naturalized governors general — from best to least in terms of effectiveness — in each category as follows: "Right Royal" — Georges Vanier, Roland Michener, Vincent Massey, Jules Léger, Ray Hnatyshyn; "Crown Legatee" — Adrienne Clarkson, Roméo LeBlanc, Jeanne Sauvé, Edward Schreyer, Michaëlle Jean. It is too early to definitely position the current occupant, David Johnston.

the stuff of footnotes (even my footnotes), and it deserves to be read and reread wherever and whenever the need arises to understand who we are. When I reread it, I also think of Ken Wiwa's tribute to Adrienne Clarkson as governor general,[28] and remember the unique way she evoked the country and the sense of pride I felt in her governorship. So here's Adrienne Clarkson's "Eulogy for Canada's Unknown Soldier," delivered in Ottawa on Sunday, May 28, 2000:

> Wars are as old as history. Over two thousand years ago, Herodotus wrote, "In peace, sons bury their fathers; in war, fathers bury their sons." Today, we are gathered together as one, to bury someone's son. The only certainty about him is that he was young. If death is a debt we all must pay, he paid before he owed it.
>
> We do not know whose son he was. We do not know his name. We do not know if he was a

---

[28] Wiwa, the son of the executed Nigerian patriot Ken Saro-Wiwa, worked out of Massey College when he wrote the tribute to Madam Clarkson in his *Globe and Mail* column. I remember him bringing it to me first and asking if I thought it was "over the top." I said it wasn't, and I also noted that only an outsider from Africa would be allowed to make such a statement, as a Canadian would be roasted alive. Wiwa wrote that the fact that "Adrienne Clarkson, once a refugee, represents the Queen here in Canada is, for me, the singular most important reason for believing the monarchy is relevant to Canada's emerging identity. Her role may only be ceremonial and symbolic, but as the enduring quality of the Royal Family attests, you can never underestimate the power of myth."

JOHN FRASER

MacPherson or a Chartrand. He could have been a
Kaminski or a Swiftarrow. We do not know if he was
a father himself. We do not know if his mother or
wife received that telegram with the words "Missing
In Action" typed with electrifying clarity on the
anonymous piece of paper. We do not know whether
he had begun truly to live his life as a truck driver or
a scientist, a miner or a teacher, a farmer, or a student.
We do not know where he came from.

Was it the Prairies, whose rolling sinuous curves
recall a certain kind of eternity?

Was he someone who loved our lakes and knew
them from a canoe?

Was he someone who saw the whales at the mouth
of the Saguenay?

Was he someone who hiked in the Rockies or
went sailing in the Atlantic or in the Gulf Islands?

Did he have brown eyes?

Did he know what it was to love someone and be
loved back?

Was he a father who had not seen his child?

Did he love hockey? Did he play defence?

Did he play football? Could he kick a field goal?

Did he like to fix cars? Did he dream of owning a
Buick?

Did he read poetry?

Did he get into fights?

Did he have freckles?

Did he think nobody understood him?

Did he just want to go out and have a good time with the boys?

We will never know the answers to these questions. We will never know him. But we come today to do him honour as someone who could have been all these things and now is no more. We who are left have all kinds of questions that only he could answer. And we, by this act today, are admitting with terrible finality that we will never know those answers. We cannot know him. And no honour we do him can give him the future that was destroyed when he was killed. Whatever life he could have led, whatever choices he could have made are all shuttered. They are over. We are honouring that unacceptable thing — a life stopped by doing one's duty. The end of a future, the death of dreams.

Yet we give thanks for those who were willing to sacrifice themselves and who gave their youth and their future so that we could live in peace. With their lives they ransomed our future.

We have a wealth of witnesses in Canada to describe to us the unspeakable horror and frightening maelstrom that war brings. What that first World War was like has been described in our poetry, novels, and paintings. Some of our greatest artists came out of that conflict, able to create beauty out of the hell that they had seen. The renowned member of the Group of Seven, F. H. Varley, was one of those artists. Writing in April 1918 he said:

"You in Canada . . . cannot realize at all what war is like. You must see it and live it. You must see the barren deserts war has made of once fertile coun- try . . . see the turned-up graves, see the dead on the field, freakishly mutilated — headless, legless, stomachless, a perfect body and a passive face and a broken empty skull — see your own countrymen, un- identified, thrown into a cart, their coats over them, boys digging a grave in a land of yellow slimy mud and green pools of water under a weeping sky. You must have heard the screeching shells and have the shrapnel fall around you, whistling by you — seen the results of it, seen scores of horses, bits of horses lying around in the open — in the street, and soldiers marching by these scenes as if they never knew of their presence. Until you've lived this . . . you cannot know."

It is a frightening thing for human beings to think that we could die and that no one would know to mark our grave, to say where we had come from, to say when we had been born and when exactly we died. In honouring this unknown soldier today, through this funeral and this burial, we are embracing the fact of the anonymity and saying that because we do not know him and we do not know what he could have become, he has become more than one body, more than one grave. He is an ideal. He is a symbol of all sacrifice. He is every soldier in all our wars.

Our veterans, who are here with us today, know what it is to have been in battle and to have seen their friends cut down in their youth. That is why remembrance is so necessary and yet so difficult. It is necessary because we must not forget and it is difficult because the pain is never forgotten.

And the sense of loss, what this soldier's family must have felt, is captured in a poem by Jacques Brault, the Quebec poet who lost his brother in Sicily in the Second World War, and wrote *Suite Fraternelle*:

I remember you my brother Gilles, lying forgotten in the earth of Sicily . . .

I know now that you are dead, a cold, hard lump in your throat, fear lying heavy in your belly, I still hear your twenty years swaying in the blasted July weeds . . .

There is only one name on my lips, and it is yours Gilles

You did not die in vain Gilles and you carry on through our changing seasons

And we, we carry on as well, like the laughter of waves that sweep across each tearful cove . . .

Your death gives off light, Gilles, and illuminates a brother's memories . . .

The grass grows on your tomb, Gilles, and the sand creeps up

And the nearby sea feels the pull of your death

You live on in us as you never could in yourself

You are where we will be

You open the road for us.

When a word like Sicily is heard, it reverberates with all the far countries where our youth died. When we hear Normandy, Vimy, Hong Kong, we know that what happened so far away, paradoxically, made our country and the future of our society. These young people and soldiers bought our future for us. And for that, we are eternally grateful.

Whatever dreams we have, they were shared in some measure by this man who is only unknown by name but who is known in the hearts of all Canadians by all the virtues that we respect — selflessness, honour, courage, and commitment.

We are now able to understand what was written in 1916 by the grandson of Louis Joseph Papineau, Major Talbot Papineau, who was killed two years later: "Is their sacrifice to go for nothing or will it not cement a foundation for a true Canadian nation, a Canadian nation independent in thought, independent in action, independent even in its political organization — but in spirit united for high international and humane purposes . . . "

The wars fought by Canadians in the twentieth century were not fought for the purpose of uniting Canada, but the country that emerged was forged in the smithy of sacrifice. We will not forget that.

This unknown soldier was not able to live out his allotted span of life to contribute to his country. But in giving himself totally through duty, commitment, love, and honour, he has become part of us forever. As we are part of him.

I have never known Adrienne Clarkson to be less than resolute. She has a depth of feeling for the sinews of this country that is so strong it very nearly made me believe we didn't need a Sovereign. It's a pretty important point, actually. Had she stayed in office for a decade, had she been allowed to soften some of the edges of the busy itinerary she and John Ralston Saul set themselves, had then Prime Minister Paul Martin supported her when she needed that support, the argument for retaining the Crown would have been seriously weakened.

But controversy, and the handling of controversy, is always lurking. And there were two significant and highly scrutinized controversial issues that affected the office of the governor general during the past two decades. The first was the brouhaha over the expenses involved in Adrienne Clarkson's controversial viceregal visits to northern countries, and the other was during her successor's term in office, when Michaëlle Jean had to deal with a tricky request at the end of 2009 from Prime Minister Stephen Harper for the prorogation of Parliament. Both these events have been endlessly described and analyzed. Both are interesting because they deal with real issues as they affect the role of the Crown in Canada.

Curiously, although the business of the prorogation caused the most headlines and brought out all
the Cassandras, it seemed the least complicated of the
two issues. The governor general, in this case Madame
Jean, consulted widely before she and her advisers came
to a decision. I remember the eminent University of
Toronto political scientist Professor Peter Russell fly-
ing to Ottawa on the same airplane I was on, he to be
picked up by a chauffeur and official from Rideau Hall,
and I to travel with the masses (no complaints). He was
being consulted on the prime ministerial request for
prorogation. Because there was a minority Tory administration at the time, the possibility existed that
if the government were defeated the governor general
could use her royal prerogative to summon the recently
discredited leader of the Liberal Party, Stéphane Dion,
and ask him if he could put together a coalition of the
Liberals and NDP. That would have been within her
rights, but had she done so, it would be a fair prediction
that that would have signalled the end of the viceregal
system. Putting into office a discredited leader of an
electorally rejected party, regardless of what coalition
could be put together temporarily, would have caused
a worse crisis than the famous King-Byng Affair

of 1926.[29] In the case of the 2010 prorogation "crisis," Madame Jean made the only decision that made sense, a correct decision regardless of how arrogant one might feel the prime minister had been in seeking temporarily to avoid parliamentary scrutiny.

Madam Clarkson's woes over her northern nations saga were, to me, completely different and completely distressing. She was accused of wasting public funds on "useless trips" to "useless countries." Her beautiful vision of using her office, as it had never been used before, to bring Canadian realities — thinkers, artists, writers, architects — to all the countries bordering on polar regions was something so imaginative and daring, it brought out the "Little Canada" in — of all parties — the NDP.

---

[29]   The King-Byng Affair, according to the usefully accurate gospel of Wikipedia, was "a Canadian constitutional crisis . . . when the Governor General of Canada, the Lord Byng of Vimy, refused a request by his prime minister, William Lyon Mackenzie King, to dissolve parliament and call a general election. The crisis came to redefine the role of governor general, not only in Canada but throughout the Dominions, becoming a major impetus in negotiations at Imperial Conferences held in the late 1920s that led to the adoption of the Statute of Westminster in 1931. According to British Empire constitutional convention, the governor general once represented both the sovereign in his British council and his Canadian council, but the convention had evolved with Byng's predecessors, the Canadian government, and the Canadian people, into a tradition of non-interference in Canadian political affairs on the part of the British government. After 1931, the governor general remained an important figure in Canadian governance as a constitutional watchdog, but it is one that has shed its previous imperial duties."

On top of that, she was saddled with a prime minister in Paul Martin who clearly didn't like her very much and left her in the lurch to defend herself.

Even if it was Madam Clarkson's (and John Ralston Saul's) own imaginative idea, it had been officially supported by the government, and no appointed high official should ever be abandoned like that. Not only should she have been defended publicly, we were made to look foolish in the eyes of the countries who had to be informed that the trip to such great allies as Sweden, Norway, and Denmark (plus its province of Greenland) was called off.

Because Massey College supports the Canadian Journalism Fellowship for mid-career journalists, modelled on the famous Nieman Fellowships at Harvard (also copied by the Knight-Wallace Fellowships at Ann Arbor), we are invited every year to visit several Scandinavian countries. They are always added on to the primary trip to Finland (proudly un-Scandinavian), whose officials originated the concept years ago. On the first of the two proposed trips to these northern countries, Adrienne Clarkson and John Ralston Saul had made it to Finland, and we went on our annual journalism trip a few months later. Everywhere we went in Helsinki and beyond, people told us of the impact the viceregal visit had made, more impact than any other state visit

anyone could remember. We kept running into artists and writers, journalists and parliamentarians, who
wanted us to know how much it meant to them as Finns
that Canada cared enough to send a major delegation of
such significance.[30]

Yet the other side of the equation was equally telling.
Unless the government of the day supports the viceregal
apparatus, and indeed the monarchy, it will definitely wither and fade, or — as with Madam Clarkson's
woes — be subjected to ludicrous controversy, however
unfair.

MADAM CLARKSON GOT misunderstood on this one famous occasion, just as Hilary Weston got outrageously
misunderstood when the announcement of her viceregal
appointment was made. Two years prior to the Clarkson
announcement from the Prime Minister's Office, Mrs.
Weston's wee trip on the media tumbrils duly ensued.
Anyone perusing her early clippings, post-announce-

---

[30]   On that first trip to Finland following the Clarkson viceregal visit,
it took me a while before I told Herself that one high official had said, ad-
miringly, "it was the greatest state visit to Finland since the Czar came."
I certainly never told her NDP and Liberal Party critics either, and now
both parties have other fish to fry and Adrienne Clarkson is far away
from the griddle.

ment, would be forgiven for thinking the prime minister had searched diligently to come up with the closest contemporary approximation of Marie Antoinette to become lieutenant governor of Ontario. Richard Brennan, bureau chief for Southam at Queen's Park, and also president of the Queen's Park Press Gallery, derided her as a rich man's wife and opined that if the prime minister had wanted a department store owner to be the Queen's representative in Ontario, he would have been better to have appointed "Honest Ed" Mirvish. John Gray of the *Globe and Mail* selectively quoted her to make her sound like a cross between the English comedian Joyce Grenfell and a parody of the Queen herself. Allan Fotheringham, the self-appointed Junius of the *Sun* tabloid chain, and Margaret Wente, the Madame Defarge of the *Globe and Mail*, both slagged her in their distinctive styles.[31]

---

[31] "I would like to extend my sincere thanks to the Prime Minister for this brilliant appointment," wrote Ms. Wente. "Hilary Weston will be a shining example to the ordinary women of this province. And I would like to thank Mrs. Weston, in advance, for the sacrifices she is about to make in the name of duty. She will, for example, have to step aside from her job as deputy chairwoman of Holt Renfrew. I just hope she can get those third-floor dressing rooms remodelled before she goes. The ones at the Bloor and Yonge store. They really are quite tacky." Allan Fotheringham, on the other hand, couldn't get over the thought of how uncomfortable it would be for Hilary Weston to be handing out certificates of merit to miners in Sudbury and sitting down to tea with working wives in Hamilton. Both Ms. Wente and Mr. Fotheringham wrote, one presumes, from their extensive experience of living amongst the ordinary folk of

It is always a shock to someone unused to extensive media coverage how distorted their own image becomes. I have always been amused by an old joke which begins with a question, "Why are journalists and lawyers so hated and despised?" and the answer is "because you haven't worked with an architect yet." What is anthropologically intriguing about the joke is that the professionals from all three occupations are, essentially, con artists. The lawyer tells the client he will keep him out of jail, which is small comfort when behind bars with the fees still to be paid. The architect says he is going to build your dream house or building, but it turns out to be *his* dream house or building and costs three times as much as he said it would. The journalist is the only one *not* after your loot. He says he wants to tell your story to the world, but when the story comes out in print it turns out not to be your story, but his interpretation of your story, and your reputation is destroyed in the carefully balanced nuances of the tale ("on the one hand, Mr. X is known for his courtesy and charm; on the other hand, his reputation for miserliness is unequalled and makes Scrooge seem a regular Andrew Carnegie . . .").

Ontario. Ms. Wente has been spied, at least once, accepting help from a waitress in handling a coffee machine at her place of employment, and I know for a fact that Mr. Fotheringham is never loath to get opinions from taxi drivers.

So Mrs. Weston was hit by fully loaded guns on all sides. She had to take a big gulp and decide, from resources deep within her — aided by weathering successfully the tough time she had in Ireland as the eldest daughter in a fatherless family — that all these snide commentators weren't going to do her in. She then proceeded to be the Queen's representative with the skills and means that she had. If she lacked experience, she went out humbly and trained herself. She didn't need her salary, so she donated it to a cause she also fought for during her five years in office — youth unemployment and other youth issues. She quietly brought comfort to the afflicted and great dignity to her office, without overspending. The Weston sense of identification with the homeless attracted media attention, and the way she reached out to a wide variety of endeavours of altruistic young people was genuinely inspirational. She was industrious and charming, and modelled herself — or so it seemed to me — somewhere between the Queen and Princess Diana. She also made sure she had great staff, and her all-important secretary, Richard Berthelsen, worked tirelessly at making sure the public and the government understood exactly how important she and her office were.

And when all the media dust and chicken feathers had settled to the ground, it was widely acknowledged she'd done a star turn. "How could I have been so snide?" wrote Margaret Wente in 2002, as Mrs. Weston was about to step down from her high office. "Mrs. Weston is the real thing." The left-of-centre *Toronto Star* eulogized her and, all in all, she could be forgiven — as she noted in her own memoirs, *No Ordinary Time* — for thinking she had been translated from Marie Antoinette to Mother Teresa. She was neither, of course, and she also learned a lot:

"Despite its historic roots and symbolic importance," she wrote in that memoir, "the office of lieutenant governor is a fragile institution, constantly threatened by misunderstanding, outdatedness, or mockery. I was to learn that preserving a tradition does not mean pickling it, and that the best way to maintain the authority and dignity of the office is to keep it responsive and relevant."

AFTER MRS. WESTON stepped down, Ontario's first aboriginal lieutenant governor was appointed. This was the Honourable James Bartleman. He identified himself and his viceregal mandate with, amongst other good causes, First Nations literacy, and used his office to ram the point home to the entire province — and beyond. This was through a donation project that saw the transfer of tens of thousands of books to First Nations school and community libraries. Yet the best use made of the lieutenant governor's role in the long and arduous process of reconciling the First Nations with the larger society came thanks to a brave initiative of Bartleman's successor, the Honourable David Onley.

Onley has been paralyzed for most of his life thanks to infant poliomyelitis, and he came to be identified with "disability issues." But he also became the first lieutenant governor in any province who adopted and maintained his predecessor's goals (the literacy project), and who then built on those goals by using his honourable old office as part of the means of helping to heal wounds associated with the residential school abuses issue. He did this with the only power a viceregal figure has wholly at his or her disposal: through symbolism and identifying his office and person with a cause.

So it happened one fine October day that many of Ontario's great and good and utterly surprised traipsed up to the Queen's Park audience chamber of the representative of the Sovereign and found themselves watching and participating in a truth and reconciliation session with David Onley. He inhaled sacred tobacco, he listened to some truly ghastly stories, and he showed how decent Canadians, with good intentions, can display useful solidarity with a long-beleaguered people. Did it solve all the problems? *Hardly.* Did the mainstream mass media pick up the story and spread it widely so that a larger population could see what was being done? *Ha!* Did it make a difference? *Yes, it did.* And not just to those in attendance. It established again that the Crown has a role in bringing citizens together, a role in helping to correct ancient wrongs, a role in witnessing even when a larger population seems to remain indifferent. *This is not nothing.*

THE OFFICE OF lieutenant governor does not have to be suffused with stifling protocol. The Crown, in an appropriate or serendipitous setting, can provide a leitmotif of pugnacious levity and strong local pride. Arriving in St. John's a few years ago with an invitation to stay at the beautiful early-nineteenth-century Government House was both an honour and a source of intense curiosity. That's because the "governor"[32] of the moment is the Honourable John Carnell Crosbie, scourge of all Liberals, provincial or federal, and a man of such

---

32   There were "governors" of Newfoundland — Britain's oldest colony and for years a self-governing dominion, like Canada — right up to 1949. The title is still deployed by a certain sort of patriotic Newfoundlander, perhaps to remind mainlanders that they have a different history than Canada's prior to Confederation.

mercurial temperament you never know from one day
to the next whether you are to be buoyed up by his island nationalism or lacerated like the victims of Dame
Edna Everage, that Australian cross-dressing scourge
of all that is complacent, pompous, or pretentious in
this life.

We'd rented a car at the St. John's airport and made
our own way to central St. John's for a two-day stay
with Their Honours, John and Jane Crosbie, whom I
had known really well since my time as an undergradu-
ate at Memorial University of Newfoundland (1965–
69). We drove slowly past the security kiosk at the
main gate, but the Royal Newfoundland Constabulary
officer in charge of Their Honours' security and safety
was clearly sound asleep. Not wanting to disturb him,
we proceeded along our way, up the pleasant driveway,
and parked our car next to His Honour's (the licence
plate — a crown instead of numbers and letters — was
the giveaway). My wife and I got our overnight bags
from the trunk and walked, with appropriate gravitas,
to the main entrance.

I had been through these doors long before. First
in 1966, when the Honourable Fabian Aloysius O'Dea
was governor and the Queen Mother had come to St.
John's aboard the Royal Yacht *Britannia*. That year I had

a summer job covering the royal tour as a journalist for the *Evening Telegram,* and it was quite something to be coming back to Government House forty-five years later as the guest of the incumbent.

"Haaalllooooo," we shouted in the main entrance-way once we were inside. Dead silence. Spooky silence. Just inside the entrance, the hallway was festooned — if memory serves me right — with battle flags of the Royal Newfoundland Regiment, that brave company of young Newfoundlanders whose exploits included being slaughtered at Beaumont-Hamel during the First World War, thereby wiping out most of a generation of idealists who might have saved Newfoundland from the worst of the terrible calamities that struck the island dominion during the subsequent Great Depression.

I tried shouting louder, and this finally elicited, from far away, "Is that Johnny Fraser?" His Honour himself eventually emerged like a heavenly apparition, looking down over a balustrade which surrounded an elegant oval opening in the main entrance hall. "I thought at the very least there would be an aide-de-camp to greet and attend to us," I said in a mock affronted sort of way.

"No, b'y, we don't use an aide-de-camp for a bloody journalist. What d'you think? This is no low-life residence. Come on up. Jane and I are watching the news. None of it is good."

So up the Missus and I went into Their Honours' private quarters on the second floor. Official residences are not quite as wonderful as they may seem from the outside or in the imagination. The highest possible premium is put on trying to find a wee bit of space, a few rooms perhaps, where some privacy is possible. Most of the residences are public spaces for work or work-related entertainment. After a few months of maintaining a rictus smile and healing the calluses from a couple of thousand handshakes, you won't find many lieutenant governors swanning around the premises thinking, "Oh whoopee, this is all mine." You will find them, as often as not, trying to make a cozy nook where they can feel normal.

It was in that cozy nook that the Crosbies were found when we finally made it upstairs. Our bedroom suite was a gas, and it included a beautiful not-quite-king-sized bed with the Royal Arms carved into the headboard, which reared high above the bed. It had been made for the visit of Edward, Prince of Wales, in the 1920s, but he had preferred to stay in his ship's quarters, so the bed had to make do with less exalted fry like the Missus and meself (as they say locally in St. John's).

First thing Monday morning, though, His Honour was up and off and running in a schedule that would have exhausted men half his age. He was hosting an official lunch, but before that he was making an official visit to a school just outside St. John's, which was celebrating its centenary, and he had to get back not just for the lunch but also for a session with Labrador fishermen who wanted to consult him unofficially on some trouble "up the way." In the evening, he and Her Honour were off to a special presentation at the Arts and Culture Centre. The day we left Government House for a trip up the shore to Salvage, on Bonavista Bay, the viceregal pair were off to St. Anthony, on Newfoundland's spectacular northern arm (where Gros Morne National Park is located), and then to Labrador to honour an anniversary of the Grenfell Mission hospital operations on the island and its vast mainland territory.

I couldn't figure out when the incessant round let up, and — frankly — I don't think John Crosbie could either. He gave no complaint except, perhaps, about Danny Williams — then the premier — and his studied inability to understand that the lieutenant governor has the right "to be consulted, to warn, and to encourage," in the famous language of Walter Bagehot. ("Danny only likes the 'encourage' part," His Honour divulges.) But viceregals no less than Royals accustom themselves to the constant round and earn their keep a hundred times over.

It is a curious thing, is it not, that viceregal appointments have generally anticipated public elections? We had to have a female (Jeanne Sauvé) appointed governor general before we managed a female prime minister (Kim Campbell). In the provinces, prime ministers — supported by the Queen — have made major advancements in breaking through barriers of race and gender in the highest appointments. Consider: we have now had fifteen female lieutenant governors since 1974; as far back as 1945, an Acadian was appointed lieutenant governor in Prince Edward Island, long before there was ever an Acadian premier; most significantly there have been five First Nations or Métis lieutenant governors,[33] outstanding Asian-Canadian and Afro-Canadian lieutenant governors, and provincial regents with visible disabilities.

---

[33] Steinhauer in Alberta, 1974; Dumont in Manitoba, 1993; Bartleman in Ontario, 2002; Point in British Columbia, 2007; and Nicholas in New Brunswick, 2009.

These adroit kinds of appointments probably did more to silence criticism of the Crown as an entity than anything else, precisely because they showed how the system could evolve and be made to reflect the reality of the nation, even more quickly than the electoral process was able to do. Out of this sort of quiet change, the system has been operating with a degree of efficiency and public comfort that defies easy analysis.

At the same time the monarchy itself continues to evolve, although the problem for the Queen and the rest of the immediate Royal Family is that "evolution" and reform are necessarily slower because the monarchy has to be streamlined with all the Queen's realms in the Commonwealth. But when the moment actually arrived, look how brilliantly it was done. In October 2011, at the Commonwealth prime ministers' conference in Australia, two of the most vexing historic roadblocks in the shared monarchy were removed, almost "just like that." One of them was the centuries-old prohibition of Royal Family members who marry Roman Catholics from remaining in the line of succession to the throne. The prohibition referred only to Roman Catholics and, of course, was tied to the old battles of the sixteenth, seventeenth, and eighteenth centuries between the state Anglican Church in England and the See of Rome. The heir to the throne could marry a Jew or a Sufi mystic if he or she wanted to, but not a poor Catholic!

Ditto for the ancient practice of making sure all the sons of a reigning monarch are accommodated in the succession before the daughters. Now, in line with the Scandinavian and Dutch monarchies, the first child to be born to the reigning monarch or his or her heir — male or female — will succeed. Long overdue in both cases, you might say, but these issues are politically and historically delicate. "First male out of the womb" may have been established as constitutional law, but that did not prevent four glorious female monarchs (and six female monarchs in total) from reigning: Queen Elizabeth I, Queen Anne, Queen Victoria, and Queen Elizabeth II. Nor did it stop the appointments of female regents in the Queen's other realms and territories.

So viceregal rule is not just a thing of the past, and the life of the Canadian regents of the "throne" at Rideau Hall is not just a constant round of diplomatic levees, official visits, and ceremonies to honour new recipients of the Order of Canada or medals for courage. Like Queen Mary, they are never bored — or at least never allow themselves to be bored — and like Queen Mary they love hospitals, and veterans, and schoolchildren, and performers of all kinds, and soldiers and teachers, and — in fact — all of us, if we are doing anything more in life than simply marking time.

CHAPTER THREE

King Charles III of Canada?

They're changing guard at Buckingham
*   Palace —*
Christopher Robin went down with Alice.
We looked for the King but he never came,
"Well, God take care of him, all the same,"
Says Alice.

They're changing guard at Buckingham
*   Palace —*
Christopher Robin went down with Alice.
They've great big parties inside the grounds.
"I wouldn't be king for a hundred pounds,"
Says Alice.

— From "Buckingham Palace," by A. A. Milne

P RINCE PHILIP WAS THE FIRST TO FIGURE IT OUT, the first to spot the signs and make the connections. Then he recorded it all grimly in his mind and never forgot it. He did all this long before his son and the heir to the throne became its principal victim, and before his grandson Prince William actually helped to catch one of the monsters and was the cause of his being sent to prison.

We are talking about journalists and writers here. The tribe. The writers of royal realities and royal fictions. Prince Philip realized when he read the first fantasy about his "failing marriage" with Queen Elizabeth[34]

---

34   Like all young married couples, Philip and Elizabeth had adjustments to make, only their adjustments had to be made under the full glare of media intrusiveness. A few years after his marriage in 1947 and the Coronation in 1953, the sorrow over his lost career in the Royal Navy and the almost total lack of privacy perhaps overwhelmed him. In any event, with the Queen's fervent approval, he was allowed to go on an extended world cruise aboard the Royal Yacht *Britannia* to do some travelling in peace that he could never do otherwise, there to figure out how

that the media was the enemy. Because he is incredibly astute, he also realized that the monarchy could not do without the media, and thus was established the terrible tension between media and monarchy that has been such a feature of the reign of Queen Elizabeth II. And it has been Prince Philip, more than any other member of the Royal Family, who has given vent to the frustrations this arouses. For the better part of seven decades, he has been supporting the Queen, and if you are looking for the resilience and backbone of the contemporary monarchy, most of it can be found all along the spine of this one shrewd and very much misunderstood and underestimated man.

The misunderstanding and underestimation, for the most part, suit him, one gathers. This is partly because, early on in his marriage, he had been labelled by the popular media as a crank. It was assumed that anyone who had to walk three steps behind a woman, even a queen, must somehow be flawed, or at the very least constantly frustrated. That's because royalty correspondents and lesser journalistic fry are forever projecting their own fantasies onto the central figures of the

_____

to handle the rest of his life, a life he had pledged to his wife and Sovereign. The speculation about a marriage breakup — completely manufactured — continued until they were happily back together again, several months later. Then it was time to go after Princess Margaret again.

Crown. Sometimes they are right, but mostly they are so wrong they have to build an entire edifice of conflict and pop psychology (and lies) to sustain the concocted myth of the month.

The fact, the simple fact, is that instead of being frustrated with his role, it is Prince Philip more than anyone who has steered the Royal Family through the stormy and uncertain weather that marks our era, in which all deference to position and status is far gone and unelected aristocrats seem perpetually to be readying themselves for a ride to oblivion. Time and again throughout Queen Elizabeth's reign, it will emerge that it was her consort who pushed for something which in retrospect took the Family Firm to a better vantage point or rescued them from a dangerous precipice, whether by allowing cameras into some of their private lives, thereby risking a de-escalation of the mystery and reverence which "crowds the head that wears the crown," or by creating a regular and informal internal discussion about "the way forward" for the monarchy.

Much as he may deplore the reality, it was Prince Philip who understood faster than anyone that the age of deference was over and the Royal Family had to get with the times if it was to continue serving its better purposes. That was why it was Philip who first pinpointed the danger and challenges the Firm was up against with the media in general and the Murdoch press in particular. He realized that a sort of cancer had emerged in the more populist newspapers, which weren't just out to embarrass the monarchy but were more than content to see it hounded into extinction. This insightful and strategic thinker is not at all the Prince Philip the world knows. That guy is the politically incorrect and crotchety old boy who is forever causing the Queen minor embarrassments, like the time he told a British graduate student in the People's Republic of China who was wearing a Mao jacket that if he stayed much longer in the Middle Kingdom he might develop "squinty eyes." There has never been anything anodyne or faceless about the Duke of Edinburgh, and his caustic one-liners are much more fun to write about and blow up than any boring reality.

At Massey College in Toronto, where I work and reside, we got a chance to have a brief but close-up look at Prince Philip's style, thanks to his great friendship with our founder. At Mr. Massey's request, he agreed to lay the cornerstone of the college in 1962. Forty years later, in 2002, during the Queen's Golden Jubilee tour of Canada, he agreed to return to Massey College — as the representative of the Royal Family and as Chancellor of the University of Cambridge — to help us celebrate our own anniversary and also to become the college's first Honorary Senior Fellow. He was on the college's premises for not much more than an hour, but during that brief period — which had taken close to five months of planning — he had disarmed just about everyone he met. He even charmed the one group he went out of his way to insult — the journalists.

Massey College's Canadian Journalism Fellowship welcomes outstanding mid-career journalists to spend an academic year away from their jobs, to refresh themselves, and to try to become better journalists. Positions are much competed for. As I was touring Prince Philip around our college quadrangle, we came across the journalists, neatly collected into a cadre under their supervisor, Professor Emeritus Abraham Rotstein, the eminent political economist.

For years, Prince Philip has put up with the slings and arrows of the media. They have been out stalking him and his family for every single tidbit of scandal or trouble they can find or manufacture. He has read many times about the imminent end of his own marriage; he has read about countless affairs he never had; he has read about his hatred for Princess Diana, whom he worked so hard to embrace; he has read about his constant dismay about his eldest son and heir to the throne, as if his was the only family in the entire history of the world that has not had to deal with conflict with its eldest offspring. He has seen the whole apparatus of the Royal Family depicted as corrupt and corrupting, of "infantalising" government and the general population, of being part of the "wretched social baggage" of keeping people in their places and helping the rich get richer, as parasites on the body politic. The list goes on and on. Mostly he never responds, but sometimes his bark emerges:

"Well, sir," I said, as I was about to introduce him to the journalists, "here are the journalism fellows."

He stopped on his heels, almost like the Road Runner suddenly facing Wile E. Coyote. "And what do they do?" he asked. The tone was definitely menacing.

"Well, sir, they get a subsidized academic year off from work to study whatever they want. They get to go on trips to study foreign countries and institutions — "

The sentence was never finished before he pounced.

"Sounds like a bit of a holiday, is it then, chaps?"

"Yes, sir," they all said, almost deferentially.

"Bit of a holiday for your victims too, I'll wager."

And then he was off. He wasn't going to waste any more time *there*!

An equally amusing and abrasive echo of that

meeting occurred almost ten years later as he celebrated his ninetieth birthday on the eve of the Queen's
Diamond Jubilee:

"Well, sir," said the BBC interviewer, trying to start
gently with the dotty old royal personage before getting
into the obligatory insulting questions, "you are about to
celebrate your ninetieth birthday."

"Well done!" Philip said in mock tribute to her accu-
racy, and he had her on the defensive for the rest of the
interview. In the old days, he would have been skewered
for the contempt he clearly expressed. At ninety, he can
get away with it and, in any event, he couldn't care less.
His story is out there and people can make of it what
they will. Before he quits this earthly scene, he has also
had the presumably immense satisfaction of seeing the
High Miscreants of the reign of Elizabeth II brought to
the court of judicial and public opinion, thanks to the
Murdoch press hacking scandal, duly unfolding even
as I write these words. Prince Philip always understood
how unfair the media game could be and he also knows
exactly for whom his life has been in service and what
it was all about. Only once in public has the Queen acknowledged it, but it was — from her — the most crucial acknowledgement in her life, almost on par with her
Coronation oaths:

"He is someone who doesn't take easily to compliments," the Queen said of her husband during a Guildhall luncheon in 1997 to celebrate their golden wedding anniversary. "He has, quite simply, been my strength and stay all these years, and I, and his whole family, and this and many other countries, owe him a debt greater than he would ever claim or we shall ever know."

I thought of the Queen's compliment as I toured Prince Philip around our college during that Golden Jubilee year of 2002, watching family, dear friends, and colleagues transform in his presence. Partly, of course, it was due to the proximity to such a famous face; partly it was the chance, in a small way, to see our own lives criss-crossing with a bit of history; but it was also partly the unexpected warmth and charm of a man who had been depicted often as a politically incorrect sub-monster. His public image had been selectively isolated, with all his panache removed. It was his panache, more than anything, which people warmed to on that sunlit autumn day in our quadrangle, that and his unerring instinct to reach out to anyone exuding friendship or respect, whether it was a member of the kitchen staff or the most venerable and honoured academic in our midst. If they were prepared to carry on the great game with him, he was prepared to play, and in the way he has ensured that the Royal Family still has a role amongst us.

On the eve of his ninetieth birthday, the *Spectator* got it exactly right. After noting all the thousands of things he has done and the causes he has supported, the editors pointed out that in 1953 he had knelt before the Queen during her Coronation and promised to be her "liegeman of life and limb" and to "live and die for her."

"For six decades," the article concluded, "he has stood by those vows . . . In his quiet way, the Prince helps keep alive old-fashioned virtues of duty, courage, forbearance, and public service. These have been the lifeblood of what is arguably the most successful monarchy in the world."

PRINCE PHILIP'S DARKEST suspicions about the media, mixed in with Prince Charles's worst public moments and Prince William's astute assumptions, all came to an astonishing denouement during the royal tour of the Duke and Duchess of Cambridge in July 2011. While they kayaked, helicoptered, horse-drawn-carriaged, and generally charmed their way across Canada, the *News of the World* phone-hacking drama unfolded in Britain. The tour was not exactly overshadowed by the developing revelations, but it certainly did feed into them, and not the least reason for this was what Prince William himself precipitated nearly six years earlier, when he realized the ghouls from the *News of the World* were hacking his own phone calls and messages. Court officials went to the police, and four years later Clive Goodman, the *News of the World*'s "royal editor," was sent to prison, abandoned by his colleagues and superiors as a "rogue" journalist. Almost before Prince William went back to Britain after the Canadian royal tour, he was to learn that some members from the Diplomatic Protection Group of the London Metropolitan Police had accepted bribes to hand over private cellphone numbers of the Royal Family.

For years, as Prince Philip's acerbic comment to the journalism fellows at my college in 2002 testified, the Royal Family have been victims of the Murdoch press and its tabloid copycats. So powerful was this boisterous Australian press lord that he had the prime ministers of both the Labour and Conservative administrations pay court to him. Indeed, whenever an election approached, he was arguably much more powerful than either PM. He clearly encouraged the era of disrespect for members of the Royal Family because their star quality and foibles were such good fodder for his wretched newspapers and their compliant readers.

A sting operation was successfully mounted on the

wife of the Queen's youngest son, Prince Edward, whose public relations business was quickly closed down as a result. Even more spectacularly, as we have seen, the divorced and economically desperate Sarah Ferguson was caught taking a bag of cash, with the promise of more, for "access" she had agreed to arrange to her ex-husband, Prince Andrew. These silly lesser Royals were easily fooled dupes, easy pickings for the unscrupulous *News of the World.*

In any event, the public went along with all this because the victims were politicians, sport and media celebrities, and royalty: in other words, people whose feelings and privacy are irrelevant in today's world. The "public" feels a price must be paid for celebrity status, and that price is their privacy.[35] Only when the Murdoch

---

35   The ruthlessness of the ghouls who worked at the *News of the World* should not be underestimated. A senior psychiatrist at a leading Canadian hospital, who was born and trained in London before emigrating with his family to Canada, recently told me a typical story. During his residency in the late 1980s under an eminent psychiatrist, a senior reporter from the *News of the World* contacted him discreetly and told him that they had solid information that Princess Diana was seeing a psychiatrist and they believed it was his supervisor. "I wouldn't know," said my informant, "as my supervisor doesn't see his private patients at the hospital." Yes, pressed the reporter, but we want you to look at his schedule. "Why would I do that?" he asked indignantly. "Because you would not like to see what we would publish about what you have been up to," came the startling answer. "But I have done nothing wrong," he said, again indignantly. "Perhaps. But we suspect that you cannot afford

press started listening in on phone calls and messages left for and by the families of victims of murder and terrorism did the public finally get it. It's not just whatever problem young Prince Harry might be experiencing that is so delightful to read about and have a chuckle over; it's also your own little five minutes of celebrity, should something untoward happen to you or those near to you, that catapults you into momentary fame or notoriety. That's when people (and advertisers in the newspapers) finally understood that they themselves bore some responsibility for the degeneration of integrity and civility, and were even indirectly complicit in the criminality of phone hacking.

In all of the miserable and illegal intrusions against the Royal Family, nothing exceeded the eavesdropping on the intimate and now "notorious" conversation Prince Charles had with his future wife, Camilla Parker-Bowles. It occurred in 1989, after his marriage to Princess Diana had irretrievably broken down and they were both seeing other people.

---

to disprove what we will write about you if you don't help us." My informant, an anti-monarchist, felt sufficiently threatened to check that schedule, found nothing, and managed to worm his way out of trouble. I didn't question his meek acquiescence because we now know if he had informed the police about this blatant act of extortion, the police — already corrupted by the Murdoch forces — might have duly reported him to the *News of the World* editors.

The marriage, to quote the Princess of Wales's famous observation, was indeed "crowded," but not just with Camilla. Diana herself had a succession of lovers. Camilla was the only woman Charles had truly loved, but, sadly, he had to abandon her on the stern advice of mentors[36] and marry the woman he was urged to marry because she was more "appropriate" for an heir to the throne. It was a mismatch and nothing could change that, no matter how hard both Charles and Diana tried to make it work. And they did try, regardless of the fantastic lies you may have read or heard concerning the early years of the marriage.

According to Charles's official biographer, Jonathan Dimbleby, it was out of the depths of loneliness and despair that the old relationship with Camilla was reignited. That is the human context of the conversation, and any couple that has gone through the harrowing business of a breakup will understand exactly what was going on and also how mean-spirited the hacking and publication of the conversation was. You can listen to it, or read it, for yourself thanks to the ever-present Internet,[37] but if you do, maybe some small corner of

---

[36]   His father, Prince Philip, and his uncle, Lord Mountbatten.

[37]   Just go to your friendly Google gossip service and punch in "Prince Charles + Camilla + cell phone conversation."

your heart might also recall intimate conversations you yourself have had with your spouse or lover and imagine them touted about the media and Internet.

Uncomfortable as I felt reading the fundamentally innocuous dialogue, I also found it strangely moving as a depiction of two lovers, lonely and lost, struggling to survive the heavy and often gruesome complications of their lives. I also wondered where the two of them found the courage to do so. I also remember, following a trip Charles and Diana made to Canada in the 1990s, my beloved old editor-in-chief of the *Globe and Mail*, Richard J. Doyle, saying he noticed an "ambience of erosion" in the relationship at a dinner for the royal couple at Rideau Hall, and he felt sorry for both of them. "Don't ever let anyone fool you into thinking it must be fun being royal," Dic Doyle — who by then had been appointed to the Senate of Canada — said to me later. "It's a prison, and you could see it in her trapped eyes and in his solemn if despairing resignation."

In another era, of course, a royal mismatch would have been dealt with behind closed doors. They both could have had their extra relationships and done the proper thing in public — just like Charles's great-great-grandparents, King Edward VII and Queen Alexandra did[38] — and the great unwashed public would have known nothing of it for decades. Instead, we know more about this failed marriage than any other failed marriage on God's earth, and the only good I can think that came of it all is that it showed everyone else going through marriage strain that nobody was exempt. In the end, the Royal Family is still a family, even if a dysfunctional family from time to time, like our own families. I think this makes them seem closer to us and more human. If any of us had our own relationships put under the kind of scrutiny the Prince of Wales has to suffer, if we had hackers listening to either our most amorous or most rancorous conversations — in flushes of desire or moments of anger — we would be hard-pressed to be

---

38   Famously, we now know, Edward VII's "longest-serving" and last mistress, Alice Keppel, was also the great-grandmother of the Duchess of Cornwall. In Gyles Brandreth's 2006 study of Charles and Camilla (*Portrait of a Love Affair*, Arrow Books), King Edward is depicted enjoying the ordinary domesticity of life in Mrs. Keppel's household, "kindly allowing her children, who called him 'kingy,' to race slices of buttered toast down his trouser leg." Queen Alexandra, thanks to the customs of the day, was not allowed the privilege of a lover, and the crumbs from her buttered toast were merely "warm relationships" with courtiers and her dogs. In the little dog cemetery on the grounds of Marlborough House near Buckingham Palace (now the headquarters for the Commonwealth Secretariat, but for some years prior the retirement home for Alexandra in her widowhood), there is a wee stone memorial for "Mr. Jiggs, faithful friend to Queen Alexandra for seventeen years" — sadly more faithful than her husband, the King-Emperor.

as disciplined and forbearing as Prince Charles. He is a good man, much maligned and much underestimated.

Throughout most of his adult life, Prince Charles, heir to the throne and King the moment his mother, the Queen, dies and hands on the hereditary torch, has been the principal victim of the media royalty mania. He has been subjected to more ridicule, innuendo, outright fabrication, and grotesque invasion of privacy than almost any other individual alive today. Part of the problem, of course, is that he has opinions that some people disagree with. An equal part of the problem is that the women in the House of Windsor live a long time, and he has been in the waiting line longer than any heir to the throne in history.

The longevity of the Windsor women is not a joke, at least not to him. His beloved Scottish grandmother, Queen Elizabeth, the wife of King George VI, ruled our hearts much longer as the Queen Mother than she ever did as Queen Consort, and lived on till she was past her century. Charles's own mother, our Queen, looks set to break even that record. Since he was born in 1948 and the Queen won't reach her centenary until 2026 and, say, we give her two years of grace following that epochal moment, Charles can look forward to wearing the Imperial State Crown round about 2028 or 2029, at the ample age of eighty or eighty-one. His enemies wonder if he winces when loyalists say, "Long live the Queen," which shows how little they understand Prince Charles. His flaws, both those that are real and those that are imagined but nevertheless widely ascribed to him, have been trotted out so often and for so long that most people haven't any real and tangible idea who he really is.

Everything that is decent and good about Prince Charles comes as a shock to those who insist he is a crank or a wonk or a wuss or a doofus or a whatever. His skill at athletics, his bravery during assassination attempts (check out Google for the one in Australia in 1994 if you want a definition of sang-froid), his prophetic wisdom about ecology, his genius as a loving and wise father, his careful aim at arrogant professionals (like architects who enjoy obliterating or desecrating monuments of the past such as the National Gallery in London or the Royal Ontario Museum in Toronto), his astuteness as a businessman, his support of corporate responsibility, his effectiveness in fighting social inertia amongst the young and unemployed, his inspired ability to transcend religious differences and animosity, his dutifulness to his mother and Sovereign: whenever you hear about these qualities Charles possesses, they always seem to be presented as a footnote to a portrait of either an idiot savant (at best) or — more typically — a meddling, dangerous fool. And still he waits and waits.

Not once, however, has Prince Charles ever complained about the wait — nor even hinted at the frustration of being perpetually second in line. Vice-presidents in the United States can hardly take being in such invidious succession for four years, let alone two terms. In Communist China or the old Soviet Union, to be second in line — under Chairman Mao or Comrade Stalin — was usually a death sentence. Charles is a human being, and we know, from both his friendly and unfriendly biographers, that he has had periods of despondency, but it has not been because he is not yet King, it is because he is subject to the normal range of emotions we all are, in his case attached to the specifics of his fate. He did not wake up one day in his boyhood and suddenly say: "Yippee, I am going to be King" and then spend the rest of his days wondering when that day would be. There was a gradual awareness that a heavy duty had been laid upon his shoulders, and eventually he discovered that part of the weight was that there would also be a long wait.

That's also why, a long time ago, he clearly came to the obvious realization that he would be Prince of Wales, the traditional title for the male heir of the monarch going back to the fourteenth century, for decades, and King for only a few years. And with that realization came the decision that it would be as the heir to the throne, rather than as someone seated upon it, that he would have to make his mark in the span of his lifetime. And the mark has been impressive and quite moving, although so many people who have not followed what he has been trying to do dismiss it all, often with contempt. It is, as I say, one of the most extreme examples of people getting someone almost completely wrong, and often getting him wrong with such assured passion and ostensible inside information that one wonders if they are directly related to the Lord Chamberlain. But no, it is usually something they have heard discussed, or overheard, or got secondhand — usually originating in the Murdoch press.

But the long wait gave Charles more freedom to pursue his interests and causes, and to speak out about them. It has also allowed all the doubters, nitpickers, naysayers, and the rest of the sour brigade amongst the commentariat to pick away at his role, his person, his dreams, and all his solid achievements, along with whatever turmoil and errors are also part of his life, as they are a part of everyone's lives. As Shakespeare's Henry V duly observes, he has been subject to "the breath of every fool."[39]

So LET US start with the indictment against the Crown: first from Britain and then from Canada, because there is no point to the Canadian constitutional monarchy if it is built on an unstable foundation and future in Britain. We do not "borrow" the British monarchy for our head of state, but we do share it, and we came by the sharing honestly through history and volition and convenience. Here then are excerpts from a savage attack on the Prince of Wales penned by Max Hastings, former editor-in-chief of the *Daily Telegraph* (when Conrad Black was

---

39   KING HENRY, prior to the Battle of Agincourt:

> *Upon the king! Let us our lives, our souls,*
> *Our debts, our careful wives,*
> *Our children, and our sins, lay on the king!*
> *We must bear all. O hard condition!*
> *Twin-born with greatness, subject to the breath*
> *Of every fool, whose sense no more can feel*
> *But his own wringing! What infinite heart's-ease*
> *Must kings neglect that private men enjoy!*
> *And what have kings that privates have not too,*
> *Save ceremony, save general ceremony?*

proprietor), but in this case published in London's *Daily Mail* in December 2010, under the headline "Why Prince Charles is too dangerous to be king: In a landmark essay Max Hastings tells why this increasingly eccentric royal could imperil the monarchy." It begins pianissimo, but the crescendo is not long in coming and was occasioned by the publication of the Prince of Wales's new book, titled *Harmony*. In it, Charles opines on a number of issues he has for a long time considered important, such as our misuse of the natural eco-culture of the planet, our abandonment of any metaphysical analysis of what ails humankind, and our mechanistic acceptance of all purported "advances" in science.

The wedding of William and Catherine "will be a big success," Max Hastings assures us, but then goes on to add that as the Queen gets older, growing attention and speculation is focusing on the monarchy's future. Pretty soon, he's aiming for the jugular. Charles takes on causes that reject the evidence of science (holistic medicine, for example), he meddles in the professions (architecture), he rejects the traditional roles of the monarch (his position within the Church of England):

"He is not a bad man," Hastings concedes, "but I think he is a very dangerous one for the monarchy, if allowed to ascend the throne. I remain apprehensive that his eagerness to become King derives from hopes of using the position to promote his dotty causes ... The best hope for the future is to maintain the Queen's great tradition, of being all things to all her subjects by remaining a smiling, but silent, monarch. In the days when royal advisers occasionally sought my opinions as a newspaper editor, my counsel was always the same: 'Say nothing, say nothing, say nothing...'"

Well, Hastings goes on (and on) and represents a pretty consistent minority High Tory view of concern in Britain about any public figure, elected or appointed or anointed, who holds forth on views different than their own. But he also sets the mainstream media tone for poor Charles, as well as the critical response to his recently published book. Journalists are nothing if they are not cheerful lifters of other ideas (myself included), so it wasn't surprising to find the *Globe and Mail's* usually astute man in London, Doug Saunders, reshuffling many of the anecdotes and apocrypha from this and other articles in the British media for a pre-nuptial swipe at the monarchy and Prince Charles in particular.

Wrote Saunders in the *Globe*: "Whether you happen to enjoy or abhor any of Charles's ideas (and those who embrace all of them are a small community), the important message of *Harmony* is that he considers them his calling. His ideology is not just a personal faith but a mission, and he intends to use all his resources to make it everyone's ideology, not just in Britain but throughout the Commonwealth . . ."

It is hard to know where to start with all this busy traffic. Well, with Hastings, it is not at all true that the Queen never lets on what she is thinking. What she doesn't do is publicly make trouble, but that approach has also landed her with the charge of irrelevancy. The Britain and Canada of the early part of Queen Elizabeth's reign were dramatically different from the Britain and Canada of today. In both countries, for example, multi-racial and multicultural realities have become a major component of public thinking and government legislation. Prince Charles, in essence, has done what the early attacks on the Queen advised her to do, which was to take on a more contemporary involvement in society and the life around him. If King Edward VIII had not flown the coop with his Yankee bride but had continued along the line he had started espousing when he publicly expressed his deep concern about the plight of the unemployed in Depression-ravaged Britain, a Max Hastings of the time would have described him as dangerous too.

Nor is it true that there are not many people who believe in the causes the Prince of Wales espouses. There are, in fact, millions who do. They may not see the degradation of the planet in exactly the same light and with the same degree of concern that Charles does, but his early insight — for which an extraordinary amount of abuse was heaped on him — was accurate and the start of a wake-up call for all of us. In Canada, there would be many more people on his side than against him on this issue. But what is especially depressing in the attacks on Prince Charles is the shallowness of the research and insight, coupled with what the observers always feel is the irrefutable logic of calling for the end of the monarchy.[40]

To me, there are only two legitimate questions here. Is it for certain that Charles will succeed to the throne

40   A good example is the vicious attacks on Charles for his support of "integrated" medicine. He has never said anything other than to give alternative methods a look before dismissing them, and that drives some Western medical practitioners wild with anger, although if any profession should know that it is as much an art as a science it should be the medical profession. But, just as Prince Charles's "unacceptable and eccentric views" on the ecosystem of the planet are now everyone's religion, so in the new age of unaffordable medicine are alternative solutions coming into their own. In the July issue of *The Atlantic*, for example, the major feature touted on the cover is "The Triumph of New-Age Medicine," and the come-on blurb atop the actual article states: "Medicine has long decried acupuncture, homeopathy, and the like as dangerous nonsense that preys on the gullible. Again and again, carefully controlled studies have shown alternative medicine to work no better than a placebo. But now many doctors admit that alternative medicine often seems to do a better job of making patients well, and at a much lower cost, than mainstream care — and they are trying to learn from it."

and be King of Canada? And the other obvious one is: what kind of king will he be?

IN A THOUGHTFUL column written at about the same time as the priggish Max Hastings wrote his "landmark" essay in London's *Daily Mail*, Michael Valpy noted in the Toronto *Globe and Mail* that the success of the royal tour of Prince William and his bride had brought about commentary to the effect that it would be great if we could bypass Prince Charles as the heir to the throne and go straight to William.

"William and Kate are swell," wrote Valpy. "They're young; they're comely. They're baggage-free, a signal accomplishment given their eight years of being hunted by the depraved British news media. There's no mark on them."

Valpy goes on to point out that "in our throw-away, hyper-obsolescence culture, talk in the Queen's realms has been turning to skipping the next genera-tion — throwing away old and weird Prince Charles from the line of succession — and going straight to Prince William when his grandmother lays down the torch . . . The current charge against [Charles] is that his public policy advocacies go too far beyond the limits of constitutional permissibility for him to be acceptable as a sovereign. So junk him."

Constitutional monarchy, Valpy continues, is not a beauty contest and does not require a pop star or a rocket scientist. "It requires someone committed to the job. The Queen, when she became Queen at 25, pledged to commit her life to the people whose sovereign she was. She has done that . . . No one doubts that Charles would make the same pledge . . . Charles has been trained for the job of sovereign since birth. He's obviously socially compassionate. His interests are the leading issues of the day. That answers the question of whether he'll make a good king."

But exactly what kind of a good king? It's worth looking at the way Prince Charles has gone about arousing some of the controversies for which he is so famous, if not notorious. Usually they tell you much more about the naysayers and complainers than about himself. His life is much more than an open book: it is an entirely exposed encyclopedia. The first thing it is important to understand is that if he has used his position of prominence to speak out on issues that inflame some observers, he is far from being the dilettante the media so often accuses him of being. He has researched and thought deeply about issues as well as using his position to consult widely and distinctively. More than any other member of the Royal Family, he understands the multicultural and multiracial world we all now find ourselves in. He has also looked deeply into the stresses of life for ordinary citizens, especially those squeezed into council housing in Britain, and he feels a compulsion to investigate and, where he thinks it important, to speak out. Contrary to Max Hastings, Prince Charles does understand the restraints of his position and the parameters of the permissible. He's just not prepared to accept other people's definitions of those parameters, and when he speaks out, it is usually after long consultation and brooding.

Let me anatomize one instance that might have bypassed most people in Canada — and which makes it useful, because we might be able to have a better perspective on it. In some circles in Britain, it caused near hysteria. A few years ago, when Prince Charles was talking about some of the antique constitutional paraphernalia and baggage he must carry along with his title and fate, he humbly suggested that he would prefer the title "Defender of Faith" rather than the traditional title of "Defender of the Faith," which all British sovereigns take on at their succession and coronation. He dropped one word. The word "the." The firestorm of controversy which ensued said much about the challenges Charles faces all the time, trying both to remain true to himself and to nudge the monarchy more fully into contemporary life. For me, somewhat selfishly, it is a really interesting issue because it brings in history, religious hypocrisy, and the mysterious element of the metaphysical into the tale, and those are all areas of inquiry I love poking a stick into. It's a failing, if you like, but there it is, and so please bear with me. There is a legitimate and pertinent point to be made here.

When Charles becomes King, in Britain he also becomes head of both the Church of England (Anglican) and the Church of Scotland (Presbyterian). None of this affects the Canadian branches of those Christian denominations, but it is perhaps more than passingly interesting to note that the title "Defender of the Faith" (or "Fidei Defensor" in the original Latin) was bestowed by a pope (Leo X) on Henry VIII in gratitude for his loyalty to the Roman Catholic Church! This was in 1521, at least five wives and a religious revolution before relations between the Holy See and the Throne of England took on a different hue. The title remained because the kings and queens of England claimed the headship of their church in England (and later, under the Stuarts, in Scotland) and have to attest to this reality in their coronation oaths.

For most people today, this is all other-worldly or completely silly, but it is tied up with constitutional issues in Britain, and it is significant to those who believe that a spiritual dimension in our lives is important.

This is what Charles actually said in a 1994 British Independent Television documentary on his role as heir:

> All the great prophets, all the great thinkers, all those who have achieved an awareness of the aspects of life which lie beneath the surface, all have shown the same understanding of the universe or the nature of God or the purpose of our existence — and that is why I think it is so important to understand the common threads which link us all in one great and important tapestry . . .

Although a devout practising Christian, Charles has looked deeply into other religions and has found these parallels not just amongst the three "prophetic" religions (Judaism, Christianity, and Islam) but also in the Eastern religions of Buddhism and Hinduism. He has also watched the growth of multi-faith societies in Britain, Canada, and many of the Queen's other realms, and that led him inexorably to look at the exclusivity of the Coronation oath, which requires the Sovereign to take on not just the headship of the "established" Church of England and Church of Scotland but also that title "Defender of *the* Faith." Here's more of what he said during the television interview:

> I personally would much rather see it as "Defender of Faith," not *the* faith, because it [Defender of the Faith] means just one particular interpretation of the Faith, which I think is sometimes something that causes a great deal of problem — has done so for hundreds of years. People have fought each other to the death over these things, which seems to me a peculiar waste of people's energy, when we are all actually aiming for the same ultimate goal, I think. So I would much rather it was seen as defending faith itself, which is so often under so much threat in our day where, you know, the whole concept of faith or belief in anything beyond this existence, beyond life itself, is considered old-fashioned and irrelevant. [41]

41   Here comes an offbeat "full disclosure" moment, because this perfectly coincides with my own metaphysical views. I do not like to be cut off from any possibilities. At Massey College, where I work and reside, there is a College Prayer — penned initially by Robertson Davies for an all-male college and somewhat rejigged by me to accommodate the other half of humanity at a coeducational college. It is on the choir wall of St. Catherine's Chapel under the Latin quote from Erasmus, via Horace, that was the personal credo of Carl Jung, who had it carved over the portal of his front door: VOCATUS ATQUE NON VOCATUS DEUS ADERIT (Called or not called, God is present), and here is the prayer: *"Beloved God, you have in your wisdom placed in the minds of men and women a pure principle*

Although not hitherto known for its defence of matters of faith, the media were quick to pounce and — in fairness — they had help from all the usual suspects. My favourite was the then Archbishop of Canterbury, the spiritual leader of the Church of England, Dr. George Carey, who was from the "Low Church" tradition of Anglicanism, which takes a somewhat fundamentalist approach to church tradition, practice, scriptural interpretation, and theology. There is a history of troubled relations between English sovereigns and archbishops of Canterbury. Thomas Becket and King Henry II, of course, ended in the murder of "that meddlesome priest" in 1170. Thomas Cranmer was burned at the stake under orders of Queen Mary I in 1556, and Charles's great uncle, King Edward VIII, was harangued about his lifestyle from the pulpit of Archbishop Cosmo Lang in 1936. So it was an old tale renewed when Archbishop Carey took it upon himself to "explain" to the world what the heir to the throne was *really* saying. This particular meddlesome

---

which in different places and ages has had different names, but which we know proceeds from you. It is deep, and inward, confined to no religion, nor excluded from anywhere the heart stands in perfect sincerity. Wherever this takes root and grows, a community is nourished. Grant, our God and Mentor, that all who are accepted in fellowship at this College in search of wisdom in this world, may also find your wisdom, and that the children of this House may be united through you in their courage, inquiry and mutual concern. AMEN."

prelate said that what Charles had meant to say was that he really did want to be "Defender of the Christian Faith" but that he "didn't have the opportunity to express his fully formed views." What the Prince was intending, continued His Grace, "was perfectly compatible with being 'Defender of *the* Faith.' As heir he has to be concerned with every citizen, regardless of creed and colour."

Prince Charles, at this point, decided to keep his mouth shut publicly, although it has been noted that the "dialogue" continues and the stance he took resonated with much of a religiously sidelined population in Britain. But no one who follows these sorts of debate was in any doubt what the Prince actually thought,[42] and many also thought he was brave to begin the public discussion. Others — the Max Hastingses of the world — thought him utterly daft.

---

[42]   Charles expanded on his theme in the ITV interview, but the continuation never made the final cut. According to his biographer, Jonathan Dimbleby, he went on to say: "I feel that certainly the great Middle Eastern religions — Judaism, Islam, Christianity — all stemming from the same geographical area — all have a great deal in common. And I think Christianity had a great deal more in common a long time ago than it does now — sadly in my opinion ... A lot of that is due to the great schism between the Orthodox Church and the Roman Church before the Reformation produced Protestantism. I also think there are aspects of Hinduism and Buddhism, again further east, which are attached by very profound threads to Islam, Christianity and Judaism. And when you begin to look at what these religions are saying, you find that so much of the wisdom that is represented within these religions coincides ..."

For me, this all came home in a dazzling speech he made while I was writing these words — on July 5, 2011. In a speech far more "landmark" than anything in Max Hastings's tiny universe, Prince Charles addressed the 250th anniversary of the Board of Deputies of British Jews at the historic Guildhall in London. Charles pointed out the gradually progressive but not untroubled history of Jews in England and noted continuing issues of anti-Semitism and lack of regard for all the great gifts Jews have brought to the principal realm. He traced the good and bad in this history and told a never-before-heard anecdote about Prince Philip, at a boys' school in Germany during the rise of Nazism, defending a Jewish schoolmate from vicious bullying. The thrust of the speech was to push the Royal Family right into the vortex of Jewish, Christian, and Muslim relationships in his future realms and to show that even in an age of declining faith, the role of religion positively guided has major contributions to make:

"It is fashionable to say that 'modern Britain' is a patchwork of many different faiths and many different communities," he said in his peroration. "That is certainly true, but I have always thought it a little misleading to suggest that it was ever any different! When our country has drawn strength from diversity it has been literally world-beating. It is only when we have allowed difference to gnaw away at us or when we have tried to extinguish difference, as in the fifteenth and sixteenth centuries, that we have been weakened at home and abroad.[43] So the importance of 'Unity through Diversity' cannot be overstated. We do not all share the same faith, but we should not forget that we are linked by faith itself, sustaining and enriching our national life. In the various charitable initiatives I have tried to inspire or champion over the years, I have believed passionately that each faith, with its rich ethical and spiritual base, has a crucial part to play in promoting the harmonious tolerance that is the bedrock of our society. Each faith, of course, draws on a profound belief in the sanctity of human life. I recall your own Jewish exhortation in the Book of Deuteronomy: 'Choose life!' I am also reminded of the welcome the Patriarch Abraham gave, so many thousands of years ago, to three strangers, running to meet them, and inviting them to rest at his home and strengthen themselves with his food. Kindness was the way of Abraham; the path, according to your fine tradition, to true spirituality."

---

43   Most of the audience at the Board of Deputies' 250th anniversary dinner celebration would have known that this was a reference to the long period when Jews were expelled from Britain and barred from entry.

The forces of organized religion are not going to rise or fall based on the sincere questioning of a prince; they rise and fall based on their appeal to the hearts and minds of the faithful and faithless alike. "The heart has its reasons which reason knows nothing of," wrote Blaise Pascal famously. To be true to himself, the Prince of Wales expressed the notions of his heart with humility and sincerity. Also with some courage. For me, that adds up to a brave man, someone to look up to, someone to be inspired by, someone who is able to transcend his malefactors and keep struggling towards the light and away from the dark. A man no longer young, but quite possibly someone who has become a man for all seasons, someone approaching Geoffrey Chaucer's "very parfitt gentle Knight."

ON JANUARY 21, 1993, Prince Charles wrote to Tom Shebbeare, then the director of the Prince's Trust, which oversees so many of the extraordinary institutions Prince Charles has founded, guided, and financed (through the funds generated by the Duchy of Cornwall and the various small- and medium-sized businesses he has built up).[44] The note is included in the sensitive

---

44   Prince Charles started the Prince's Trust in 1976, and even his detractors (including Max Hastings) acknowledge its originality and genius

biography written by Jonathan Dimbleby in 1994, written and published during some of the lowest moments in the prince's life, when his marriage had collapsed and the Murdoch brigade were going after him with hammer and tongs. It is as close to a raison d'être as I can find for the man and it seems a pretty good one, even if it was written during a period of some despair. It is focused on Britain in its specifics, but it speaks to the larger framework he tries to operate within:

> For the past fifteen years I have been entirely motivated by a desperate desire to put the "Great" back into Great Britain. Everything I have tried to do — all the projects, speeches, schemes, etc. — have been with this end in mind. And none of it has worked, as you can see too obviously! In order to put the "great" back I have always felt it was vital to bring people together, and I begin to realize that the one advantage my position has over everyone else's is that I can act as a catalyst to help produce a better and more balanced response to various problems. I have no "political" agenda — only a desire to see people achieve

---

in sparking new opportunities for disadvantaged youth. Other than the proof it offers of Charles's vision and steadfastness, the specifics of the Prince's Trust are not particularly pertinent to this tale, but do yourself a favour and check it out. The official website is www.princes-trust.org.uk, and the Wikipedia entry provides a good overview and history.

their potential; and to be decently housed in a decent, civilized environment that respects the cultural and vernacular character of the nation; to see this country's real talents (especially inventiveness and engineering skills) put to the best use in the best interests of the country and the world (at present they are disgracefully wasted through lack of co-ordination and strategic thinking); to retain the value of the infrastructure and the cultural integrity of rural communities (where they still exist) because of the vital role they play in the very framework of the nation and the care and management of the countryside; to value and nurture the highest standards of military integrity and professionalism as displayed by our armed forces, because of the role they play in an insurance scheme in the case of disaster; and to value and retain our uniquely special broadcasting standards which are renowned throughout the world.

The other point is that I have always wanted to roll back some of the ludicrous frontiers of the sixties in terms of education, architecture, art, music, and literature, not to mention agriculture. Having read this through, no wonder they want to destroy me, or get rid of me . . .

Charles had written this somewhat despondent note to the head of his Trust to rally his closest associates after a series of setbacks, notably his failed marriage, which further fuelled the hostility of his critics and detractors, all gleefully reported by the tabloid and even the serious media. Yet he stayed his course, and it has been nearly two decades since this was penned, which was before Princess Diana was killed in the Paris tunnel, before his marriage to the Duchess of Cornwall, before his mother's Golden Jubilee, before his son and heir's triumphant marriage: before a lot of good things that came into his public and private lives. The attacks continue, but I think he now has the measure of them all, and if they — his critics — have not yet figured out that the prince is not for turning, or burning, they never will.

But what of Canada? What would he be like as King of Canada? Well, what has he been like? Nothing from any of his royal tours and short-haul trips suggests he would be anything other than a good king. Yet for some time now, certainly a couple of decades, successive Canadian administrations have seemed to try to keep their distance from him. If there was distancing from the Queen herself, the *froideur* reserved for her heir was more than simply chilling. We found one excuse after another to keep him off our shores. On the occasions when he came, either on a private visit or when he was finally allowed to come with the Duchess, on a trip practically designed to keep him away from the people and places that would have ensured a successful visit, he nevertheless charmed everyone who had a chance to meet him, with both his kindness and his courtesy, but above all with his intelligent curiosity.

I met him on two occasions during the immediate past period. One was at an event organized largely by Toronto admirers that included an exhibition of young Ontario artists and was set in the charmingly *comme il faut* surroundings of the historic Gooderham and Worts Distillery District. It was a toss-up which was more surprising: people's excitement at being in proximity to royalty, or the amazement that Prince Charles was not the loon they had read about.[45]

The official trip Charles and Camilla made, in 2009, was quite low profile and caused many Canadian commentators to conclude that the monarchy was on its last legs. I remember talking to a Hamilton, Ontario, radio interviewer who ranted on about the dismal turnout when the Prince and Duchess came to look at Dundurn

---

45 When his elder son, Prince William, dazzled Canadians with the sincerity with which he greeted strangers and the consideration he gave to everyone who crossed his path, I wonder if anyone realized it was more than his mother's DNA at work. It takes two people to make a human being, and William has as much of Charles coursing through his veins and cerebellum as he does of Diana. No one who has met Prince Charles is in any doubt about the kindness of heart of the father or the son.

Castle. It was a rainy day on a tour organized by Canadian officials who thought it might be fun for the Duchess to visit a place built by a distant relative and for which no advance preparations were made for schools or historical societies to meet the royal couple.

I met Charles, briefly, during the last trip. It was at the vast reception tendered by the government of Ontario at the Carlu, in downtown Toronto. The list of invitees included far too many provincial civil servants, plus a few other likely suspects (I guess, myself included). But noticeably absent were representatives of organizations that he knows particularly well and is interested in. Still, Charles and Camilla did their duty beautifully.

I knew one young civil servant, or at least I vaguely remembered him after he came up to me and rather gleefully pointed out that I had been his Sunday school teacher at St. Clement's Anglican Church in Toronto. We were thus in the midst of a kind of reunion when the Prince was suddenly about to reach us as he was being perambulated around the large room. My former student, brasher even than me, got to shake his hand first and then introduced me to Charles by saying I had been his Sunday school teacher. A hilarious discussion then ensued about the state of Sunday schools in Toronto (dismal) and about how good a teacher I might have been (or not), and concluded with a sweet compliment about working in such beleaguered barricades of the faith.

I thought to myself, well, if he's prepared to put up with dismal receptions like this, prepared to talk to superannuated Sunday school teachers, prepared to take on the whole business of appreciating Canadians for whatever honest endeavours or voluntary work they do, prepared to speak out on issues that he feels need some special attention because they will affect all of us, then he will do very nicely as a king of Canada. His own outlook on the world is dramatically different from that of, say, Prime Minister Stephen Harper, but that in itself seems to me a plus and an argument to put up against those who think the Harper administration's championing of the monarchy will identify the institution with partisan politics. I think Prince Charles, as King, would know exactly how to handle all this, and I also think we'd be lucky to have him and he'd be lucky to have us.

CHAPTER FOUR

Long to Reign
Over Us

Just come of age
I met her eyes
Wide in surprise
To have been
Just made a Queen
On a front page
Forty years later
Looking at her
All see the Crown
Some their mother
One his wife
Some their life

— Ted Hughes, then Poet Laureate, on the occasion of the fortieth anniversary of the Queen's Accession to the throne, in 1992

I WANT TO GO BACK NOW TO UPPER CANADA, TO Canada-before-we-became-what-we-are. When George III's long reign came to an end in 1820, and after his fickle son the wastrel Prince of Wales was crowned King George IV and then died childless a decade later, the younger brother Prince William — also childless — took over the throne and "ruled" for a scant seven years, until 1837. That's the year we are going to fast-forward to right now. Our interlocutor is Anna Brownell Jameson, redoubtable spouse of the Attorney-General of Upper Canada (as Ontario was once known). Mrs. Jameson, who kept a smart and evocative diary, was on a "summer ramble" with a small group of friends and officials on Georgian Bay and heading towards Manitoulin Island for a rendezvous with colonial and aboriginal authorities.

Their small sailboat took an historic route that also involved future signposts, because it followed Samuel de

Champlain's voyages two centuries earlier and, although this is fanciful on my part, I am sure she travelled right past where former governor general Adrienne Clarkson and her husband, John Ralston Saul, now escape to their summer cottage. I am quite sure in my own mind (and in no one else's, I have to admit) that Mrs. Jameson and her party stopped over very near Madam Clarkson's freehold and picked blueberries and raspberries nearly two centuries before the first Canadian of Asian descent to be the representative of the Sovereign in Rideau Hall would pick hers.

In her very first address to Canadians as governor general in 1999, Adrienne Clarkson evoked that place with passion. It haunts her as it haunts Mrs. Jameson's diary, as it haunted the Mohawks and Iroquois hunters, as it haunted the *coureurs de bois*, as it haunted the Hudson's Bay traders, as it haunted Tom Thomson and the Group of Seven, as it haunted great poets like Douglas LePan and Margaret Atwood, as it haunts every imaginative human being, famous or obscure, who has ever set eyes upon it.

Mrs. Jameson's journey to Manitoulin is a journey not just into the Canadian wilderness, but into a concept of place that has its own inherent majesty, into an almost mythological demi-paradise where the symbolism of kingship seems as natural as the clearing view through the morning mist, or the succession of one Algonquian chief by another. Here she is, then, Anna Bronwell Jameson in her own words and well into the journey in the early summer of 1837, after fending off mosquitoes, wind, and all sorts of other weather, and spending an uncomfortable rain-drenched night in a leaky canvas tent:

> The next morning was beautiful: the sun shone brightly though the lake was yet heaving and swelling from the recent storm — altogether it was like the laughing eyes and pouting lips of a half-appeased beauty. About nine o'clock we ran down into a lovely bay, and landed to breakfast on a little lawn surrounded by high trees and a thick wood, abounding in rattlesnakes and squirrels. Luckily for us, the storm had dispersed the mosquitoes
>
> We breakfasted in much mirth, and then we set off again. The channel widened, the sky became overcast, the wind freshened, and at length blew hard. Though this part of the lake is protected by . . . the chain of islands from the swell of the main lake, still the waves rode high, the wind increased, we were obliged to take in a reef or two of our sail, and scudded with an almost fearful rapidity before the wind. In crossing a wide, open expanse of about twenty miles, we

became all at once very silent, then very grave, then very pathetic, and at last extremely sick . . .

Daylight was just creeping up the sky, and some few stars yet out, when we bestirred ourselves, and in a very few minutes we were again afloat: we were now steering towards the south-east, where the Great Manitoolin Island [sic] was dimly discerned. There was a deep slumbrous calm all around, as if nature had not yet awoke from her night's rest: then the atmosphere began to kindle with gradual light; it grew brighter and brighter: towards the east, the lake and sky were intermingling in radiance; and then, just there, where they seemed flowing and glowing together like a bath of fire, we saw what seemed to us the huge black hull of a vessel, with masts and spars rising against the sky — but we knew not what to think or believe! As we kept on rowing in that direction, it grew more distinct, but lessened in size: it proved to be a great heavy-built schooner, painted black, which was going up against the lake against wind and current. One man was standing in her bows with an immense oar, which he slowly pulled, walking backwards and forwards; but vain seemed all his toil, for still the vessel lay like a black log, and moved not: we rode up to the side, and hailed him — "What news?"

And the answer was that William the Fourth was dead, and that Queen Victoria reigned in his place! We sat silent, looking at each other, and even in that very moment the orb of the sun rose out of the lake, and poured its beams full upon our dazzled eyes.

We asked if the governor were at the Manitoolin Island? No; he was not there; but the chief officer of the Indian department had come to represent him, and the presents were to be given out to the assembled Indians this morning. We urged the men to take their oars with spirit, and held our course due east down by the woody shores of this immense island; among fields and reeds and rushes, and almost under the shadow of the towering forests.

Meantime many thoughts came into my mind — some tears too into my eyes — not certainly for that dead king who in ripe age and in all honour was gathered to the tomb — but for that living queen, so young and fair —

"As many hopes hang on that noble head
As there hang blossoms on the boughs in May!"

And what will become of *them* — of *her!* The idea that even here, in this new world of woods and waters, amid these remote wilds, to her so utterly unknown, her power reaches and her sovereignty is acknowledged, filled me with compassionate awe. I say compassionate, for if she feel in their whole extent the liabilities of her position, alas for her! And if she feel them not! — O worse and worse!

I tried to recall her childish figure and features. I

thought over all I had heard concerning her. I thought she was not such a thing as they could make a mere pageant of; for *that* there is too much within — too little without. And what *will* they make of her? For at eighteen she will hardly make anything of them — I mean of the men and women round her. It is of the woman I think, more than of the queen; for as part of the state machinery she will do quite as well as another — better perhaps: so far her youth and sex are absolutely in her favour, or rather in our favour. If she be but simple-minded, and true-hearted, and straightforward, with the common portion of intellect — if a royal education have not blunted in her the quick perceptions and pure kind instincts of the woman — if she has only had fair play, and carries into business plain distinct notions of right and wrong — and the fine moral sense that is not to be confounded by diplomatic verbiage and expediency — she will do better for us than a whole cabinet full of cut and dried officials, with Talleyrand at the head of them. And what a fair heritage is this which has fallen to her! A land young like herself — a land of hopes — and fair, most fair! Does she know — does she care anything about it? — while hearts are beating warm for her, and voices bless her — and hands are stretched out towards her, even from these wild lake shores!

These thoughts were in my mind, or something like these, as with the aid of sail and oar we were gliding across the bay of Manitoolin.

A few nautical miles south of Manitoulin Island, on Split Rock Island in Go Home Bay, sitting in a writing cabin perched atop the Precambrian Shield and looking through a window whose view stretches all the way to Christian Island, I am writing what you are reading right now, with Mrs. Jameson's words haunting my typing.

And as I write, I also wonder about a conundrum I discovered a few years ago that still makes me shake my head in wonder at our collective historical foolishness. In Professor Donald Creighton's once-famous study of Canada's early years of nationhood, *Canada's First Century,* there is not one single indexed reference to Queen Victoria. Creighton doesn't even bother to trot out one of the few vaguely known acts of direct intervention in Canadian affairs — pointing her increasingly pudgy finger at Bytown, Ottawa-to-be, on the border of old Canada West and Canada East, on a map of her "senior realm," to try to locate a compromise capital for the proposed new experiment in federation scheduled for 1867. She's to blame for Ottawa![46]

When, in 1994, the *Dictionary of Canadian Biography* published Volume XIII, which dealt with eminent Canadians who died between the years 1901 and 1910,

---

[46] An anti-monarchist could rest his or her case right here, but, one suspects, Professor Creighton wasn't much of a jokester.

there was no biography of the old Queen. The editor's rule for making it into the dictionary, apparently, is that you have to have actually set foot on Canadian soil. In other words, even if you are the head of state of Canada, you don't make it into the official record, even if every single act of Parliament and every single law of the land was enacted or promulgated in your name. Ditto for every commission of a military officer.

If you think that is entirely appropriate, I have another conundrum for you to ponder. Guess who is the most cited name in this and the previous five volumes of the *Dictionary of Canadian Biography*. One guess only. She's listed only as "Victoria, Queen of Great Britain and Ireland." To find anything of the rich tale of Victoria's views and dealings concerning Canada, you have to go to incidental characters — like Canadian prime ministers and governors general (including her son-in-law, the Marquess of Lorne).

In this *Dictionary*, a brilliant collection of biographies but for the omission of our head of state, we can read about Sir Joseph-Philippe-René-Adolphe Caron, who was knighted by Queen Victoria. We can read lots about Baron Shaughnessy of Montreal, whose path of ennoblement began in Victoria's reign. There is Louis Riel, who was hanged in her name, and also Sir John

Thompson — our fourth (and first Roman Catholic) prime minister — who practically died in her arms at Windsor Castle, where she had just made him a privy councillor after he succeeded Sir John A. Macdonald's short-lived successor, Sir John Abbott. Although she was the titular head of the Church of England, she oversaw an elaborate Roman Catholic funeral for her Canadian prime minister before his body was returned to Canada.

This is all part of the footnote history of the secret Crown of Canada. We are a nation festooned with such "footnotes." You can read about people who founded or settled in Victoria or Regina or Jubilee or Prince Albert and still not have a clue who or what these places were named after. You can also read about three winners of the Victoria Cross — still the highest award for bravery in our country — but you cannot read a specific biography of the woman who was responsible for all of this, or in whose name decisions and awards were taken and given.

My favourite entry in Volume XIII, in which the head of state of Canada is a non-person, is that of a certain Richard Rowland Thompson, who was born in Ireland and died in Buffalo, New York. Setting foot — briefly — as a kind of remittance man in Canada after a desultory schooling in England at the end of the nineteenth century, he twiddled his thumbs for a few months before the happy reality — for him — of the onset of the Boer War. As sometimes happens, seemingly ordinary people under trying circumstances are capable of extraordinary feats (one way or another). In the case of Thompson, it was uncommon bravery. He was recommended for the Victoria Cross, which in the end he didn't receive, but he liked what he saw in South Africa so much that he went back there after the war to work for the local constabulary and, after that, in security work for De Beers Consolidated Mines (where, if we were to learn anything of his specific responsibilities, I expect we would be appalled).

There is only one reason this otherwise little man has made it into our dictionary of national biography. His singular acts of courage in the Boer War (amongst other deeds, he crossed "200 yards of bullet-swept ground to reach a wounded soldier") brought him to the attention of his Sovereign, who gave him one of four scarves she personally designed and knitted for the four bravest soldiers in her overseas dominions and colonies. Thompson was the only soldier "from" Canada to receive one. Although officially it didn't rank as high as the Victoria Cross, sentiment and the fact there were only four placed it even higher at the time. So, thanks to this scarf and a few months twiddling his thumbs in Canada before the outbreak of war, Thompson makes it into our most important history books, but the royal knitter remains excluded.

In the Creighton book, there are numerous references in Canada's first century to the "Victorian era" and "Victorian decorum" and even "Victorian imperial politics," but She who gave her name to the era makes nary an appearance. Since the book covers our first post-Confederation century — it goes up to 1967 — the only sovereigns actually mentioned are the two Georges, V and VI, and then only to note that such-and-such a prime minister trotted off to London to attend a coronation or a funeral. In the inevitable telescoping that such a popular history entails, Creighton decided, wittingly or unwittingly, that the Crown was largely irrelevant. I suppose it is also remotely conceivable that he thought the monarchy so indispensable that he didn't even think of referencing it. Somehow, I doubt it. It looks like design.

Now, contrast this familiar neglect, even contempt by omission — Creighton joins a mighty throng of national historians in largely dismissing the pertinence or any significance of the Sovereign in Canadian affairs — with Sir Wilfrid Laurier's comments to Parliament on the passing of the old Queen in 1901, five years after he assumed the premiership of the Dominion of Canada and she had been well launched into the seventh decade of her reign:

> She is now no more. No more? Nay, I boldly say she lives in the hearts of her subjects; lives in the pages of history. And as the ages revolve, as her pure profile stands more marked against the horizon of time, the verdict of posterity will ratify the judgment of those who were her subjects. She ennobled mankind; she exalted royalty. The world is better for her life.

Even if you dismiss some of the flowery language here as part of the extravagance of the era and Laurier's own romanticism, you can still detect the same sort of identification that so many people made with Princess Diana when she was killed in Paris. Unless we accept that identification amongst so many English Canadians and a fair number of French Canadians, I don't think the Victorian era in Canada can be fully comprehended, and our professional historians, frankly, have failed us badly in this as in so many other regards.

The late Sandra Gwyn, who, like Charlotte Gray today, made her name in popular social history, was one of the few late-twentieth-century writers who understood how central Victoria and the monarchy was to

Canadian affairs and Canadian life. In her remarkable book *The Private Capital: Ambition and Love in the Age of Macdonald and Laurier,* Gwyn uses as source material the practical documents of the era: newspaper and magazine articles, diaries, records of parliamentary debates, and correspondence. In all of these sources, Victoria — either personally or as Sovereign — looms almost larger than life because her personal qualities were always mixed up with symbolic roles ("Mother of the Empire," "Protectress of the Red Indians," "Defender of the Faith," and so on).

If we write Victoria out of our history by minimizing her and her role, then we continue the sense of dislocation we have in our own past, which intrudes directly on our present. Queen Victoria's role as a remote, supreme figure of Empire has a direct parallel to Queen Elizabeth's restrained and distanced role today, and for me, at any rate, it gives structure, nuance, and richness to our history and our reality.

IN HIS TRENCHANT and often amusing 2006 book *On Royalty,* the tough-minded and habitually analytical BBC journalist Jeremy Paxman — who is widely reported to fear no one — talks of his stomach quivers before meeting the Queen. Why should that be? he asks himself. Paxman isn't at all a fervent monarchist, and before he started writing his book he may well have been a republican, but by the end he could be described as a grudging monarchist. He doesn't see the point of dismantling the institution even if he feels that, starting a system of government from scratch today, the last thing one would conceive of would be a hereditary monarchy.

But the nerves? Why the nerves before meeting the Queen? I know those nerves, and just about anyone who has had the fortune to meet the Queen knows them too. They are caught up not just in proximity to celebrity, but in proximity to history and something bigger than ourselves. Almost the last thing one thinks about is the humanity of the Sovereign. We are either too busy kicking ourselves for obsequiousness or sudden catatonic shyness, or we're just making damn fools of ourselves.[47]

---

47   As I did during centennial year, 1967, when I was a student journalist for the *Evening Telegram* in St. John's, Newfoundland, and covered the reception for the visiting Queen Mother aboard the Royal Yacht *Britannia*. I had just broken up with the daughter of a provincial cabinet minister. As luck would have it, at the reception we were flung together for the first time since the acrimonious split a few days previously. We were snarling at each other when an equerry approached and said: "Oh, do come with me. Her Majesty would love to speak to some young people." I knew it would be a disaster, and as I walked towards the beaming Matriarch of Matriarchs I was pretty sure I would talk too much and also that I would get into an argument with my ex. Both things happened and,

A few years ago I managed to have close to a fifteen-minute conversation with the Queen, which according to Andy Warhol is the prescribed length of time for fleeting fame. This particular conversation was at a fairly plummy event, but nevertheless I reckoned it may well have been her three-millionth little conversation with a subject. For me, an ardent royalist, it was close to reaching nirvana. The event was private and the setting well beyond interesting. It was Fort Belvedere, a few miles from Windsor Castle, whence the Queen and Prince Philip had come. Fort Belvedere had been the home of Edward, Prince of Wales, the short-reigning King Edward VIII. It was his bolthole away from all the stuffy protocol of Buckingham Palace and Windsor Castle. It is where he wooed Mrs. Simpson, and, famously, it was where he signed his declaration of abdication in December 1936, followed by his bittersweet broadcast to the nation and the Empire. He could not endure the burden of kingship, he said, without the support of "the woman I love."

The event I attended included a magnificent fireworks display, and it was simple luck that I ended up, with my wife, standing just behind the railing of a

---

memorably, after a short, snarling exchange, the Queen Mother shushed us up with: "Children, children. This will pass. Now tell me what you are studying at university."

viewing balcony directly beside Queen Elizabeth. She nodded in our direction as the whiz-bangs were ignited and turned a couple of times to comment on a particular burst. That's when I asked her how old she was when she had first come to Fort Belvedere.

"Oh, quite young," she said. "Margaret and I loved it because there was no protocol. We had the run of the place, and my uncle had the first heated swimming pool in England. It was a sort of freedom. He was also very kind to us."

I said I had read somewhere that she was King Edward's favourite niece. "Oh," said the Queen, "that's not fair to Margaret. She was so young at the time. He didn't really know her."

She paused and then she looked at me with some intensity and said with solemnity and fervour: "What happened was a very great tragedy, you know. Very great."

Oh my God, I thought, *we are talking about the family crisis.* I was completely flummoxed and had no idea how to continue the conversation. My wife said the only time she had ever seen this happen to me was when I was interviewing the Dalai Lama at the Royal York Hotel in Toronto during one of his visits to Canada. Mercifully, the Queen turned to the person on her left.

As a huge and very loud firecracker went off, someone behind us said: "What will the neighbours say?" Being one of the closest neighbours, and indeed the landlady of Fort Belvedere, the Queen laughed out loud and turned her head: "Who said that? That's very funny."

At the end of the fireworks display, she turned to us again to say some parting pleasantry. I had recovered from my verbal inhibition and, for reasons that still mystify me, posed the following question: "My wife and I want to go to church tomorrow, Your Majesty. Can you recommend a local parish?"

She looked hard at me. I had a feeling she was trying to discern if I was joking. The silence was also a little terrifying.

"Well," I said, pushing on into the alarming void, "you're the head of my Church, and I thought you'd know the local parishes."

"I know them all," she said briskly, and then decided it was a sincere question even if, perhaps, I had spoken out of turn.

"You two better come to St. George's Chapel [the Chapel Royal at Windsor Castle, her home], but get there before 10:45 a.m., when the service starts, or they won't let you in."

With that she was off and my moment was over, ever to be cherished, at least by me. But I have brooded often about the "tragedy" of the abdication because I think I actually learned something quite important about our Queen. From many vantage points, of course, it was no tragedy at all. Most historians and contemporary observers considered Edward VIII a weak vessel and believed the nation was lucky to get Elizabeth's father, George VI, to rule it instead. You'd have a hard time finding anyone to dispute that contention, and the recent film *The King's Speech* has only confirmed it. The more I thought about her comment, though, the more I realized she may have been talking primarily about herself. She would only have been ten years old when her uncle passed on the Crown to his brother, her father, and her life changed forever. Although she was already the "heiress presumptive" before the Abdication, I believe she — like her mother — felt that the stress of monarchy helped to shorten King George's life. It definitely ended what scraps of quasi-privacy she still enjoyed. Certainly she and Prince Philip were to be denied any real lives of their own from the moment he proposed and she accepted, thanks to the instant responsibilities that were placed on her shoulders when her uncle wrote "Edward R.I."

at the foot of the historic abdication document.[48] Her father might have lived longer and, I suppose, it was conceivable that had Mrs. Simpson been thrown over, a breeding queen could have been found and Elizabeth's life would have been . . . well, it's one of those "what if" scenarios, but a fool could figure out how different her life would have been.

I believe the Queen may also have thought that if King Edward had had longer on his throne, social mores might have changed faster. Despite all the fantastic speculation about Edward's reported fascination with fascism, he was in fact an early example of a "People's Prince" and might have loosened up the staid official-dom at Buckingham Palace which so drove Prince Philip to anger and frustration two decades later.

I believe finally that the Abdication was a tragedy for Canada because Prince Edward loved our country and reported to anyone who listened — including his grouchy father, George V — that he never felt so re-laxed as he did when he was on his Alberta ranch.[49] That

48   The "R.I." is royalty Latin for *Rex et Imperator*, "King and Emperor" (of India).

49   "I want Canada to look upon me as Canadian," Edward said on his 1919 tour in Western Canada. "If I'm not actually Canadian born, I'm a Canadian in mind and spirit." It was on this hugely successful trip that he set in motion the purchase of the EP (*Edwardus Princeps* was his Latin

degree of comfort could have reflected positively on the development of the monarchy, both in Canada and in Britain. But it was not to be, and so perhaps it really was a tragedy and our Queen is as wise as I always assumed she was.

OF THE QUEEN's character, so much has been written, including in this book. Because she gives away so little that is deep within her, because exposing such a side of her character would be such a breach in the iron discipline she maintains over the outward expression of her psyche, we pundits and writers and speculators are fairly free to say and write what we want, within certain time-honoured bounds of reference, occasional deference, and ordinary observation. Two quite recent fictional

moniker) Ranch, 1,400 acres in the foothills of the Rockies, purchased at $25 an acre. In their 2011 book on royal tours in Canada, authors Arthur Bousfield and Garry Toffoli report that Edward threw himself into the work of the 1923 harvest. Wearing shabby clothes, he stooked oats, chopped sunflowers, pitched hay, and filled the silo. "I've even helped muck out the cowhouse," he told King George V. "I chop and saw the wood and I can assure you it is very hard work indeed!" At breakfast, Edward ate flapjacks and brook trout with his field hands; for lunch, corn on the cob (without utensils); and at dinner, spuds, carrots, and beets fresh from the ground. Edward kept the ranch till 1962, but one gathers his sophisticated wife, for whom he gave up "everything," was not so enamoured of mucking out the cowhouse.

treatments of the Queen show the degree of fascination it is possible to work up about her. The first is the
charming novella by Alan Bennett called *An Uncommon
Reader*, and the other, of course, is the film *The Queen*,
in which the wonderful Helen Mirren gives a convincing performance of what we think Queen Elizabeth II
must be like.

Bennett's novella speculates what would ensue if the
Queen became an avid reader.[50] The book is both saucy
and reverent, never an easy feat. Yet it makes one wrong
assumption, and it's a big one. He has put himself inside
the mind of the Queen as he imagines she would be.
Thus we get Alan Bennett being Queen Elizabeth, so
caught up in the imaginative world of fiction and cre-
ative writing that he has her realize she no longer has to
go through the unrelenting boredom of those endless levees and constitutional obligations and boring this and
boring that. That's what most of us would think if we
were suddenly and unhappily thrust into her role and
life — somewhat like Mark Twain's nineteenth-century
Yankee time traveller to the court of King Arthur.

---

[50]   In fact, she *is* an avid reader of all sorts of books (forgetting the
volumes of state papers she ploughs through every week) and has been
known to complain — to Mordecai Richler — about the amount of time
her grandchildren spend in front of "the box" instead of taking in a good
book.

Bennett also assumes that once this intellectual reality had been self-perceived, the Queen would abdicate. That is not going to happen. Monarchy is a lifetime sentence, and she prepared herself for the ordeal a long time ago.

In the twilight of her long reign, soon to be the longest in the history of this particular monarchy,[51] it is hard for any young person today to remember how young she herself was when her father died in 1952. Not even five years into her marriage and only twenty-six years old, she was thrust into a life of service very few people in the history of the world would ever have known, except perhaps mother abbesses and vestal guardians in ancient Rome. There aren't a lot of role models for queens regnant other than queens regnant: Elizabeth I and Victoria are about it, and possibly Queen Anne. The other English queens don't cut it, any more than does Catherine the Great of Russia, Queen Christina of

---

[51]   Victoria began her reign on June 20, 1837, and died on January 22, 1901, ruling for sixty-three years and 216 days. Queen Elizabeth II has reigned since February 6, 1952. At eighty-five years old in 2011, she is already the oldest reigning monarch in the history of our Crown. If, the Lord willing, she makes it to September 10, 2015, she will pass the length of Queen Victoria's epic reign, and she will be eighty-nine years old. Third on this particular list is Canada's first monarch from Great Britain, George III, who reigned from October 25, 1760, to January 29, 1820, for a total of fifty-nine years and ninety-two days, but there was a regency presided over by his son, the Prince of Wales (and future George IV) for much of the latter part of the reign, when the King was "indisposed."

Sweden, Cleopatra of the Nile, or the Queen of Sheba. Our Queen chose what we might call "Victoria lite" as her model — shorn of Empire, with the Commonwealth clinging on by its fingernails.

Soon enough after her reign began, the decline of deference for the Family Firm began, and part of the process was to expose the weaker members through media scams and scandals. And still she reigns and still she remains true to the promise she made to all of us — those of us living and those of us yet to be born — when she was still a princess. "I declare," she said in her twenty-first-birthday radio broadcast from South Africa in 1947 (to the "Empire and Commonwealth" — this was still in the 1940s), "that the whole of my life, whether it be long or short, will be devoted to your service."

Five years after this broadcast, in 1952, when her father died and most of the world found out about it before she did (she was in a treehouse in Kenya, *sans* telephone, *sans* radio, *sans* anything but the sound of the wild savannah of Africa), she was still way too young to have all the responsibility and the tedium of the contemporary constitutional throne thrust upon her and her early marriage. And she was beautifully young too, and so full of altruism and duty that those who loved her and the romance of the Crown duly ignored that shrilly upper-class

English accent that set other people's teeth on edge during the famous Christmas broadcasts, but which is undeniably hers, from "My husband and I . . ." right down to the last ". . . and God bless you on this Christmas day."

It is hard for many people, especially these days when she has become a great-grandmother, to understand precisely the nature of what she had to sacrifice to take on the mantle of Sovereign. Unlike William and Catherine, she did not experience nearly a decade of "working things out" with her future partner before they met at the altar. Our Queen was born into a world where world war was an ever-present possibility despite the horrific lessons of the First World War, when social change was just gearing up, but also when deference and the class system in Great Britain still held sway, and where racial and religious prejudice was an ordinary matter of fact in Canada. She has lived to reign into the twenty-first century, but her first Canadian prime minister — Louis St. Laurent — was born in 1882,[52] and her first British prime minister — Winston Churchill — actually participated in a nineteenth-century cavalry charge (in the Sudan, with the 21st Lancers).

---

[52] Her Canadian prime ministers, thus far, have been: Louis St. Laurent, John Diefenbaker, Lester Pearson, Pierre Trudeau, Joe Clark, John Turner, Brian Mulroney, Kim Campbell, Jean Chrétien, Paul Martin, and Stephen Harper — eleven and still counting.

Prime Minister Pierre Trudeau's famous pirouette behind the Queen's back was a gesture of rebellion after he had been excluded from a "heads of state" dinner in May 1977. As he was merely the head of government and the Queen was the official head of state, he was miffed at being excluded and actually practiced the pirouette as a non-verbal act of rebellion.

During her Silver Jubilee tour of Canada in 1977, the Queen is greeted by a salute of oars at Ottawa's Dow Lake, where a special Jubilee Regatta is being staged.

The inevitable balcony shot at Buckingham Palace of the Prince of Wales and Princess Diana after their wedding on July 29, 1981.

Head of government and head of state are happily enough rejoined in this iconic picture of Queen Elizabeth II, signing the Constitutional Proclamation on Parliament Hill in Ottawa on April 17, 1982, as Prime Minister Pierre Trudeau looks on. Canada, at last, becomes a sovereign nation — thanks to the same sovereign as before!

Above: In the happier early years of marriage, the Prince and Princess of Wales appear in Klondike style at Fort Edmonton, Alberta, in 1983
Below: Less than eight years later in, during a royal tour in Toronto in 1991, the stress and emotional weight of a failing marriage was all too clear to see.

Prince Charles has never had an easy ride as the seemingly perpetual heir to the throne. Even though the criticisms and invasions of privacy have seemed beyond reasonable endurance, he carries on. Here, on a visit to Gatineau, Quebec's Museum of Canadian Civilization in 2001, he appears to be competing for patience with a totem pole.

In Toronto on the 2001 tour, the Prince of Wales is hosted by Ontario's Lieutenant Governor Hilary Weston.

In Vancouver, British Columbia, during the 2002 Golden Jubilee tour, the Queen made a bit of personal history by dropping the puck at a pre-season NHL game in October, while hockey legend Wayne Gretzky looks on.

In October 2002, Prince Philip was made an honorary Senior Fellow of Massey College in the University of Toronto. He had laid the cornerstone of the college forty years earlier to honour his friend Vincent Massey, the college's founder. Here, the fourth Master of the College, John Fraser, listens as the Queen's consort remembers the earlier occasion.

Queen Elizabeth II is surrounded by flowers and flags during her Golden Jubilee tour in October 2002, in Fredericton, New Brunswick.

Two formidable ladies — Queen Elizabeth II and Governor General Adrienne Clarkson — arrive for a tree-planting ceremony during the Queen's Golden Jubilee tour in 2002.

Prince Charles and Governor General Michaëlle Jean wave to the crowd during welcoming ceremonies in St. John's, Newfoundland, as the Prince of Wales and Duchess of Cornwall begin an eleven-day tour of Canada in 2009.

Reviewing the troops in Toronto during the 2009 tour, the Prince of Wales is clearly more relaxed with his second wife, Camilla, Duchess of Cornwall.

The official wedding photo of Prince William, Duke of Cambridge, and Catherine, Duchess of Cambridge, came at the conclusion of one of the most successful royal liaisons in decades. The couple had a long period to get used to each other and the rigours of the official lives that lie ahead for them.

Over seventy years after his great grandparents, King George VI and Queen Elizabeth, arrived in Canada for the all-important first tour of Canada, the Duke and Duchess of Cambridge arrive in 2011 to a dramatically different country — but then they were a dramatically different couple. As Queen Elizabeth The Queen Mother once observed, "Canada made us." It made her great grandson and his bride too, especially with her maple leaf fascinator.

The Duke and Duchess of Cambridge, still dubbed "William and Kate" by the media, go in for some competitive dragon boating in Dalvay Lake, Prince Edward Island, during the 2011 tour. William embraces Kate after his team won the friendly challenge.

On July 8, 2011, the Duke and Duchess of Cambridge press the button to launch the Calgary Stampede. Their informality and ease echoed the same traits observers saw when Edward, Prince of Wales, took Alberta by storm in 1919, nearly a century earlier.

CHRIS JACKSON / GETTY IMAGES

The royal couple leave Calgary for Los Angeles at the end of a wildly successful tour of Canada. Their wedding and subsequent tours have solidified the royal couple's starring role in the new era of the monarchy — in Canada as well as the other countries where they will be constitutional monarchs some day.

She has witnessed huge changes in the world. Much of her reign was conducted during the Cold War between the forces of the West and the Soviet Union and its satellites, now part of history. Her reign is coming to its slow close as the war against Al-Qaeda terrorism continues. In Queen Victoria's day, barely forty years before Elizabeth was born in 1926, the British sent General Charles Gordon to attack the forces of the Mahdi in North Africa. In Elizabeth's time, in her ninth decade, the triumphant hunt for Osama bin Laden took place, somewhat to the east of the Mahdi's forces geographically, but proximate in terms of the world's mutual misunderstanding and inability to maintain the peace.

The major signposts of the Queen's reign are easy enough to enumerate. They start with her birth, in 1926; then, a decade later, the momentous year of 1936, the year of the three kings (her grandfather King George V died on January 20 and her uncle King Edward VIII abdicated on December 10, the same day her father, King George VI, ascended the throne); her marriage at twenty-one to Prince Philip, in 1947; the birth of her first child, a son and heir to the throne (Prince Charles), in 1948; the death of her father and her own accession to the throne, in 1952; her Coronation, in 1953; the investiture of Charles as Prince of Wales, in 1969; her Silver Jubilee, in 1977; the birth of Prince William of Wales, the second in line to the throne, in 1982; her Golden Jubilee, in 2002; her Diamond Jubilee, in 2012.

In between these junctures, of course, are lots of events and stories — great and insignificant, good and bad, funny and sad, banal and occasionally quite gripping — that have been played out in the national and international press. The glow from the Coronation didn't last all that long. The nasty stuff begins in earnest in 1957, with Lord Altrincham's celebrated attack on the "arthritic protocol" maintained by the Queen's advisers and courtiers (and her posh accent),[53] with the Canadian parallel two years later, when the CBC's Joyce Davidson had her go at the institution of the Crown and the Queen herself, in 1959. The feisty Miss (*Ms.* had not yet been invented) Davidson became, so far as I can discover, the first Canadian ever to say she was "indifferent" to an upcoming royal tour by the Queen. Those who didn't feel

---

53 "The personality conveyed by the utterances which are put into her mouth," Lord Altrincham wrote, "is that of a priggish schoolgirl, captain of the hockey team, a prefect and a recent candidate for confirmation . . . [Her style of speaking is] a pain in the neck . . . [Yet when she is older] the Queen's reputation will depend, far more than it does now, upon her personality . . . She will have to say things which people can remember and do things on her own initiative which will make people sit up and take notice."

indifferent simply howled their outrage, *a mari usque ad mare.*

The not-so-merry-go-round continues along its way to this day, and a lot of it has to do with marital unions: there were early rumours of marital discord between the Queen and Prince Philip, as a result of their first overheard argument (aboard the Royal Yacht *Britannia*); then came Princess Margaret's epochal matrimonial woes; and eventually the failure of three of the Queen's four children's marriages. All this happened during an era when marriage breakdown became run-of-the-mill and the Royal Family — if it didn't actually lead the way — at least showed it was not as dramatically different as we might have imagined.[54]

All along the long way of her reign, the Queen has had ample opportunity to show her courage. It is clearly second nature to her. In 1981, when she was on parade riding sidesaddle during the Trooping of the Colour, for

54   A quite censorious young graduate student at Massey College once told me very solemnly that the Queen and her family were "dysfunctional." I just looked at her with wild surmise and that kindly smile I try to put on when faced with the unconscious arrogance of youth: "And yours isn't?" I asked as gently as I could. She looked at me completely nonplussed. I pushed on. "I mean, I come from a classically dysfunctional family myself, and I always assumed everyone else did too, at least from time to time. But apparently you don't. I really want to meet your mum and dad when they come here next and congratulate them." She didn't laugh, alas.

example, and shots rang out, her horse — the faithful Burmese, given to her by the Royal Canadian Mounted Police[55] — looked set to bolt, but she simply steadied the beast as Prince Philip and Prince Charles both rode up beside her to offer themselves as shields. The most notorious incident was in 1982, when an intruder with the Dickensian name of Michael Fagan got into her bedroom, wielding a shard of a broken glass ashtray.[56]

---

[55] Burmese served the Queen from 1969 to 1986. She was born at the RCMP Remount Ranch at Fort Walsh, Saskatchewan, and trained at the headquarters in Ottawa. When Burmese was retired from state duties in 1986, she was put out to pasture in Windsor Great Park and died in 1990, undoubtedly the Queen's favourite horse. The Queen chose not to replace her but instead troops the colours each year in Queen Victoria's venerable phaeton (a small carriage shown on page 1 of the first insert). In 2005 in Regina, Saskatchewan, the Queen unveiled a statue of herself on Burmese outside the provincial legislature building.

[56] In Ben Pimlott's 1996 biography of Elizabeth, *The Queen*, the famous incident is reported in almost comic-opera fashion: "Early in the morning of July 9th [1982], the Queen was disturbed in her bedroom by a man who had apparently climbed into the gardens, shinned up a drainpipe, and wandered through corridors unchallenged. The intruder, Michael Fagan, drew the curtains, waking the Queen up, and began talking about his family. It took two calls by the Queen to the police switchboard before a chambermaid and a footman arrived and escorted him out. Afterwards, she told a courtier that, confronted by Fagan sitting on her bed with a bleeding hand, holding a broken ashtray, 'I got out of bed, put on my dressing gown and slippers, drew myself up to my full regal height, pointed to the door, and said "Get out!" and he didn't.' She told a friend, 'He just talked the usual sort of bilge that people talk to me on walkabout, I can handle that.' But she was not entirely nonchalant about the incident. 'I have never heard the Queen so angry,' said her footman,

Other memorable, unfunny junctures in her reign include Truncheon Saturday in Quebec (1964); the attempted kidnapping or assassination of Princess Anne (1974); the murder/assassination of her favourite uncle, Lord Mountbatten of Burma (1979); the referendum on the monarchy in Australia (1999); the fire at Windsor Castle during the famous *annus horribilis* (1992); the harrowing death of Princess Diana and the subsequent humbling of the monarchy (1997); and the troubles of Prince Andrew (even as I write, in 2011). Lots more too, the nastiest of it brought to you by the Murdoch media in its inglorious prime and then scrupulously — almost religiously — copied and followed by the "quality" media.

No other family on God's earth has been subjected to such intense scrutiny, their phone calls hacked, their police protection officers suborned for information, their "loyal" staff offered book contracts to tell all, their sex lives practically camcorded, their every scratch of the nose captured in photographs for posterity, all the off moments analyzed to utter exhaustion.

Peripherally, in any event, a lot of the Queen's life can be gleaned in visual moments via YouTube. Just go to the Royal Channel for starters and you will be led

---

who was with her when she spoke to police on the telephone from her study, after Fagan had been taken away."

to the dignified snippets, but you will in turn also be led to everything else. There's hours of it. There are several hundred books and biographies of all descriptions, thousands upon thousands of magazine profiles and newspaper articles, an Internet Niagara of *stuff*, even academic studies reporting and analyzing all the incidents, all the details, all the ups, but especially all the downs: some with a broad brush, some with ridiculously obscure intent, some true, some false, some kind and gentle, some mean and vicious, some delightfully apocryphal.[57] But for me the most poignant stopping-off point in all of this avalanche of words were the ones spoken by her in a speech made before the Lord Mayor of London's annual luncheon at the Guildhall on the occasion of the fortieth anniversary of her Accession to the throne, the same occasion for which Ted Hughes wrote that moving if somewhat bleak poem quoted at the opening of this chapter, which underscores how

---

57 I cherish two undoubtedly apocryphal tales, which I have heard so often I think of them as a royal subspecies of the urban legend phenomenon. The first has the Queen Mother opening a retirement home in Bournemouth (or Bristol or Edinburgh or Norwich), and when she finds herself with a dear old thing who clearly hasn't a clue who the Queen Mum is, she asks her gently: "My dear, do you know who I am?" The response? "No, my dear, I don't, but if you ask at the desk they'll tell you." The second has the Duke of Edinburgh in a church hall in Sudbury (or North Bay or Clarenville or Saanich) for lunch, and the waitress, picking up the empty main course plates, says: "Keep the fork, Duke. There's pie."

many of us have seen our lives set against the years Elizabeth II has sat upon her throne.

Here, in part, is what she said in 1992, and remember it was a year in which three of her children's marriages were publicly on the rocks, when her family was widely dismissed as "dysfunctional," and when her favourite residence, Windsor Castle, had sustained a devastating fire, and all of this set against a world in economic malaise and growing turmoil from the Balkans to the Middle East:

> 1992 is not a year on which I shall look back with undiluted pleasure. In the words of one of my more sympathetic correspondents, it has turned out to be an *"Annus Horribilis."* I suspect that I am not alone in thinking it so. Indeed, I suspect that there are very few people or institutions unaffected by these last months of worldwide turmoil and uncertainty. This generosity and whole-hearted kindness of the Corporation of the City to Prince Philip and me would be welcome at any time, but at this particular moment, in the aftermath of Friday's tragic fire at Windsor, it is especially so...
>
> I sometimes wonder how future generations will judge the events of this tumultuous year. I dare say that history will take a slightly more moderate view than that of some contemporary commentators.

Distance is well-known to lend enchantment, even to the less attractive views. After all, it has the inestimable advantage of hindsight.

But it can also lend an extra dimension to judgement, giving it a leavening of moderation and compassion — even of wisdom — that is sometimes lacking in the reactions of those whose task it is in life to offer instant opinions on all things great and small.

No section of the community has all the virtues, neither does any have all the vices. I am quite sure that most people try to do their jobs as best they can, even if the result is not always entirely successful. He who has never failed to reach perfection has a right to be the harshest critic.

There can be no doubt, of course, that criticism is good for people and institutions that are part of public life. No institution — City, Monarchy, whatever — should expect to be free from the scrutiny of those who give it loyalty and support, not to mention those who don't.

But we are all part of the same fabric of our national society and that scrutiny, by one part of another, can be just as effective if it is made with a touch of gentleness, good humour, and understanding.

This was after only forty years of service. As I write, we are just a few months away from the sixtieth anniversary of her Accession, and if many of her critics still find it hard to summon up "gentleness, good humour, and understanding," she herself has remained true to her Coronation vows of loyalty and faithfulness, and, as her husband has notably proclaimed, she is forbearing almost to a fault.

THIS ENORMOUS PASSAGE of time during the Queen's still active life adds an accumulated veneer to her role that is awesome and almost impenetrable. Sometimes, it is the talismans or symbols of the day that tell the tale. When I was a boy in the early 1950s, for example, you could still find in your change an occasional penny or nickel bearing the head of Queen Victoria, and Edward VIIs and George Vs were not uncommon. In Canada, there have been a total of four profile changes of the Queen on our coinage. Today it is a lucky youngster who can spot an early Elizabeth II (1953–61), and a George VI is a real treasure.

The Queen's reign in Canada also coincided almost exactly with the inauguration of Canadian-born governors general, those national regents who, along with the lieutenant governors of the ten provinces, represent the Crown in our unique and often enough peculiar — distinctively peculiar! — constitutional arrangements.

So go ahead! Can you name all the Canadian-born or naturalized governors general of Canada who have served Queen and Country in the official residence in Ottawa, Rideau Hall, since 1952? Like the number of her Canadian prime ministers, there are also eleven.[58]

She has lived so long upon her throne! In Canada, she has seen us through constitutional imbroglios, through massive waves of non-white immigration, through passionate admiration and support, through public indifference and sometimes violent contempt, and all the way back to esteem and admiration for all her constancy. In the larger world, she saw (in uniform) Britain emerge victorious from the Second World War — but impoverished, which in turn meant she also saw the steady decline of Britain as a world power and the rise of the European Community (and a diminution of her own sovereignty). She has seen the seismic shift of the economic and cultural ascendancy of the United States lead to the first intimations

---

[58] Vincent Massey, Georges Vanier, Roland Michener, Jules Léger, Edward Schreyer, Jeanne Sauvé, Raymond Hnatyshyn, Roméo LeBlanc, Adrienne Clarkson, Michaëlle Jean, David Johnston. *And here's some more crucial footnote trivia:* The names of the first Francophone and Anglophone governors of Canada are Samuel de Champlain, 1627–35 (remembered in Champlain, Quebec, and the disintegrating Champlain Bridge in Montreal) and Sir Jeffrey (later Lord) Amherst, 1760–63 (remembered in Amherst, Nova Scotia, and Amherst Island, Ontario).

of its seeming decline. She has seen both the promise and barbarism of the new Communist Chinese regime after China's humiliation and degradation at the hands of the Japanese warlords, right through to China's current economic triumph, which looms so menacingly over both Japan and the West. She's seen South Africa expelled from the Commonwealth for its racist apartheid policies, and she's welcomed it back into the fold and opened Buckingham Palace to Nelson Mandela on a state visit. She was born only half a decade after her relations in Russia were slaughtered by the victorious Communists, and she lived to see the wretched Soviet regime (somewhat) dismantled and thoroughly discredited.[59] Back again in Canada, she's celebrated with us through our own homegrown pride during

---

59   The controversy over the lack of assistance provided to the beleaguered Russian Royal Family by their British relations continues. Elizabeth's grandfather, George V, probably advised by his British prime minister, offered minimum assistance (for fear of revolutionary contamination, apparently) and may have thus contributed to their gruesome deaths. In the late 1940s, the highest-ranking survivor of the Czar's family, his aunt the Grand Duchess Olga, ended up with her two sons in a modest semi-detached home on Toronto's Delisle Avenue before moving to a farm in Halton County. It was commonly held in the neighbourhood (it was my Fraser grandparents' street) that King George (VI) had paid for the house. On the other hand, Michael Ignatieff, a grandson of the Czar's last Minister of Education, Count Pavel Ignatieff, met the Queen in Ottawa in 2010 as the Leader of Her Majesty's Loyal Opposition. Life is passing strange.

centennial year and Expo 67, seen us through that dark Canadian sense of worthlessness in the late seventies and eighties — so bad at one point that even our prime ministers sent their children to the United States for higher education — and on to a realization, as we zoom along our merry way in the twenty-first century, that we may be the luckiest nation on earth.

On the other hand, socially — thanks in part to her own family's marital squabbles — life has got less hypocritical. In 1955, three years after she became Queen, Elizabeth went through agonies trying to support her sister, Princess Margaret, when she had fallen in love with a divorced equerry at the palace, and at the same time to "rule" that Margaret could not marry a divorced man, since she was in the line of succession to the throne and the Queen was the titular head of a Church of England that didn't sanction divorce (despite its deep roots in divorce, thanks to her libidinous ancestor King Henry VIII). It wasn't just her sister and children, especially her heir, Prince Charles, who helped change the equation on the matter of marriage. Society had done all that in tandem. Indeed, society led the way, and the Queen's family was able to embrace the new norm.[60]

---

60   I realized how great the social transition was when I received a formal invitation from Ontario's "Premier Ernie Eves and [his common-law

Through all of this, through almost two dozen tours of her Canadian realm, more than to any other country inside or outside the Commonwealth, the Queen has remained constant in her duty to Canada and to that oath she made almost seven decades earlier. Through all this period, as we have seen repeatedly, she has also remained stoically responsible and steadfastly impenetrable, although her personality must surely have been subjected to more pop psychology than that of any other human being alive today. This can be safely said, thanks to the extraordinary length of her presence in the public eye. There is actually today not one person alive who can be placed parallel to her. It is speculated that she has shaken the hands of at least three million people in her lifetime, a fact that goes so far beyond any achievement in the realm of tedium that any of us can imagine. It almost raises her to the status of martyr to the public weal.

Further, it has been speculated, based on psychiatrist reports, that millions of people have dreamed about very specific encounters with her. They are invariably rather humdrum encounters: the Queen has knocked on the dreamer's front door because her driver has lost

partner] Mrs. Isabel Bassett" to join them and the Queen and Prince Philip for a 2002 Golden Jubilee reception in Toronto. Princess Margaret died a month before the Golden Jubilee officially began, so she missed the frisson of bemused satisfaction such an official invitation would have caused.

his way; another dreamer has stumbled across her in a hospital corridor; she's turned up just in time for tea; she rescues a child's dog (possibly a corgi, who knows?); she comforts a graduate student who failed to get his term paper in on time (*that's me actually*: no kidding, and while sympathetic, she was briskly no-nonsense about "getting on" with it). There are academic studies of these brief imaginary encounters with Elizabeth II, and you can even go to the Internet and have your dream of meeting the Queen analyzed for you. Indeed, you can almost be ranked hierarchically by the importance of your fantasy (my own wouldn't have rated even a C, because it was entirely self-mollifying; altruistic dreams, in which you rescue the Queen from an assassination attempt or extricate her from an awkward situation, get As). I wouldn't be surprised, although it is entirely fanciful on my part, if when the Queen dreams — in an empathetic reprise of the famous lyrics from Lerner and Loewe's *Camelot* — she is dreaming about close encounters with "the simple folk."[61]

The Queen's Diamond Jubilee will be not just a moment in history; it will be a juncture point for millions of

---

61   GUENEVERE: *What else do the simple folk do? To help them escape when they're blue.* ARTHUR: *They sit around and wonder what royal folk do. That's what simple folk do.* GUENEVERE: *Oh no, really?* ARTHUR: *I have it on the best authority.*

people throughout the rest of their lives, whether or not they love and esteem her. They will be telling their children and grandchildren and great-grandchildren that they remember the time when the old Queen celebrated her sixtieth year on the throne. There is someone alive today, possibly someone born between 2000 and 2005, who will make it into the twenty-second century and will be able to tell someone that he or she remembers his parents talking about Queen Elizabeth during the year they celebrated her long reign. If the Queen lives as long as her mother, who died in 2002 at the age of 101, she will have reigned for over seventy years, and we will have the first ever Platinum Jubilee on our hands in 2022.

So, in the end, it's the endurance that concentrates the mind here. Queen Elizabeth of 1953 is still Queen Elizabeth in 2012. The whole point of a "royal family" is that it is a family, and to realize that this remarkable woman's entire life has been played out in the public's possession is both daunting and strangely reassuring, all at the same time. Darling baby, pretty and polite little girl, dutiful preteen, wartime teen and young woman, blushing but very serious bride, young wife, grieving daughter, youthful monarch, mother times four, grandmother and great-grandmother, maybe even Queen

Mother before her days are done on earth. The endurance becomes the glue that has held everything together during tumultuous times, trumping all the negativity, erasing most doubts about the Crown, compensating for the decline in deference, easing the transition to her successors, holding the fort, bending in the wind: grab a cliché for endurance and our Queen embraces it, upholds it, embellishes it — *Lord!* she almost sanctifies it. That changing face on the Canadian coinage turns out to be the symbol of our own lives spent during the Elizabethan years, and in this saga we have our own roles to play where we transect her endurance and longevity, because it is very unlikely that any of us alive today will live out another reign anything like this one.

CHAPTER FIVE

The Once and Future Crown

"I'm going home to Canada tomorrow."

— The Queen, in 1983, on the eve of her depar-
ture for Vancouver from California

QUITE CLEARLY, IF YOU AND I SAT DOWN TO CREATE a system of government for a Canada, based on our knowledge of the ups and downs of our past, we would probably not create the system we have now. Inevitably, we would think that we could do better. We would not have a monarchy — borrowed, evolved, clipped, or truncated. You could not possibly conceive from scratch the eccentric, romantic, compromised, and too often misunderstood and convoluted institution which now nominally surmounts our constitutional and evolutionary settlement. We would certainly not have an appointed Senate. We probably wouldn't have first-past-the-post elected Members of Parliament in the House of Commons. No one sensible would have let Prince Edward Island be a province. We might well be unilingual, and even if we maintained a bilingual state, we would make sure there was such an equitable

185

arrangement of powers between the central and the regional governments that the ensuing harmony would make a Quaker prayer meeting look rancorous. The First Nations population would have its own House of Assembly, harmoniously blended with the provincial legislatures and an equal partner at all major conferences. What else? No viceregal appointments, for sure, and everyone would be responsible to someone for their ethical conduct. Every man, woman, and child would be his or her own sovereign. Honour would come naturally to those to whom honour was due. Dislocations — like murder, assault, or theft — would be seen for the mental lapses or aberrations that they are, and appropriate institutions would be developed to reprogram the perpetrator-victims. And yes, Virginia, there would also be lollipops for everyone each Thursday afternoon.

Till the dawn of this day of the New Jerusalem, however, we have what we have. The Crown, the Canadian Crown, the Maple Crown — whatever you want to call it — exists and, on a day-to-day basis, works quite well. Not perfectly, perhaps, but more than well enough. Carefully laid out constitutional strategies that are impervious to the pesky realities of the human condition have, so far as I know, been most successfully created by grotesque totalitarian states where the reality of governance has nothing whatsoever to do with the constitution's articles and codicils. The People's Republic of China has a spectacularly ethical one, exceeded only by those of North Korea and Zimbabwe. The constitution of the United States of America, on the other hand, which has been such a model for so many countries since its creation at the end of the eighteenth century, is also a magnificent document, and on one level has stood the test of time because it is rooted in the will of a free people, or at least — as originally conceived — rooted in the will of a free white male population.[62]

Yet it has often struck me as curious that the model the American revolutionaries struck upon for their head of state was that of the very Hanoverian monarch with whom they were so keen to be disassociated. In fact, in quite a real sense, Americans keep re-electing George III every four years. He was the model upon which the presidency was created. The powers of an American president today — from directly appointing all his senior and junior cabinet officers to the ability to prepare a declaration of war without immediate recourse to an elected legislature — are the powers of George III.

---

[62] As Samuel Johnson once pointed out during the period leading up to the independence of the American colonies: "Why is it that we hear the loudest yelps for liberty amongst the drivers of Negroes?"

True, there are controls, but there were on George III too: U.S. presidents and Hanoverian monarchs can and could conjure up war almost at will, but ultimately they both had to go to the "lower" legislative house to get the loot to pay for the war — either the House of Commons or the House of Representatives. Not surprisingly, the Americans never foresaw the evolution of the parliamentary system, where ministers would not only be responsible to an elected legislature but actually had to get elected to the electorate's legislative chamber, or at the very least and only in rare cases, be appointed to an "upper" house (the Senate in Canada's parliamentary system, or the House of Lords in Britain's).

The calcified power of the American presidency, glaring when caught out by majority opposing parties or factions in the elected chambers, corresponds almost exactly to the calcified power of the British monarchy by the end of the eighteenth and beginning of the nineteenth centuries. To some Canadians, the presence of a monarch as a head of state suggests static constitutional development, yet our constitutional monarchy is living, breathing proof that the evolutionary nature of parliamentary democracy is dramatically present in every act of legislation. Officially, the legislation cannot be passed definitively until the Sovereign, or the Sovereign's representative, signs it, but the Sovereign must sign what the elected legislature asks him or her to sign: there's no choice, by evolutionary constitutional tradition and by long-established practice. When the Queen or the governor general of Canada approves legislation, it is far more than a token salute to the remnants of history: it is definitive proof of the power of the people's legislature, and thus of the people themselves. When a U.S. president vetoes a piece of legislation passed by both Houses of Congress, it is very close to an eighteenth-century royal veto the particular will of the people is very hard to identify. It is, in fact, an unholy mess.

The hereditary principle, which upsets many people, seems to me to be a blessing. We embrace our historical links and eliminate any worry about the succession because it simply happens, just like that. The famous proclamation "The King is dead, long live the King" is deployed not because God says so, or a foreign power says so, or because the forces of history say so. It is because we the people in Canada say so; we will it to happen that way. Further on, it is the prime minister of the administration we have elected to govern the country who decides who will be the Sovereign's representative in Rideau Hall and in the provincial offices of lieutenant governors. So, although these are appointed officials, they are appointed through the will of the people, and that fact alone has ensured that appointed public figures have actually been more representative of society's variety than elected officials have been. Members of minorities, in particular, have been able to shine and provide genuine leadership based on this principle. The plenitude of examples tells the story better than I can. These viceregal institutions work so well that we rarely think about them, and sometimes when we do think about them a bit, we make such flip and superficial judgments, it is terrifying how closely we skirt chaos and disaster. The truth of the matter is that by some evolutionary constitutional miracle directly attributable to the presence of the Crown, we have found an official and constitutional way to include minorities of every description in the national and regional life of the country.

More than skirting chaos, though, we sell ourselves so short in Canada. We sell ourselves so short and so often it is sometimes a wonder we have any sense of who we are. Right now, as I write, Canada as a country — set in the contemporary global economic and political universe — is sitting so pretty in so many regards we hardly know our luck. Whether or not you support the current federal government, or the provincial or civic administrations in your part of the country, the fact remains that

Canada in the summer of 2011 is about the best place in the world to be living. It won't always be like this, and we still have many challenges to surmount, not the least being our historic failure to adequately reconcile our rhetoric and highest aspirations to the reality of ab-original life and the fate of the First Nations. However uncomfortable it makes us feel, however far removed we are from being able to do something directly about it, we Canadians remain liable to the charge of racism. It is one of the reasons why the attention always paid by royalty to the aboriginal population remains one of its greatest services to Canada. We forget this challenge at our peril.

Even so, we are still sitting pretty, and is it in spite of our evolved parliamentary and constitutional sys-tem? Is it in spite of the constitutional monarchy? Is it in spite of the gentle, compromising, and unrevolution-ary ways we went about creating the lives we lead and the democratic system we live under? What is it about our past achievement that helped us to be what we are today? What are the things we must shed from our past if we are to aspire to be something better than what we already are, without eradicating what helped us be-come the best place on earth in the summer of 2011? Just like my wonderful Junior Fellow who was absolutely mystified by the excitement generated by William and Catherine on their first royal tour of Canada and said "I don't get it," I don't get the concept that what has worked so well in the past, and continues to work so well, needs to be jettisoned. I think exactly the opposite. I think it should be honoured and cherished and protected.

When I have to debate the issue, it brings out the small-c conservative in me, as I am constantly reminded by detractors. It's not the worst charge in the world, and believe me, I am not abandoning medicare! Nevertheless, I am very suspicious of change for change's sake. When I look at history in my amateur and no doubt superficial way, I often see people screwing up just as we do today. Most of all, I see people trying to set the stage for results that sometimes turn out exactly the opposite of what was intended. When the American revolutionaries and the framers of their constitution set out to create their great nation, for example, they wanted a weak central government and strong states. It never worked very well, ultimately bringing them a civil war of notorious brutality, and then — almost inevitably — a ferociously strong central government and very weak state administrations.

Looking into the dreadful vortex of the American Civil War, the Canadian Fathers of Confederation made damn sure that the new federal government they were creating would be strong and the provinces as weak as possible. Good job: now we have one of the weakest central governments in the West, and the strongest regional fiefdoms.[63] The law of unintended results seems to be more constant and more consistent than almost anything else in human relations. It is perhaps useful to remember this basic rule. It is much like the one I was taught by the great University of Toronto professor emerita Ursula Franklin, Companion of the Order of Canada, survivor of the Holocaust, winner of the Pearson Medal of Peace, pacifist, and into her tenth

---

[63] When I was posted to the People's Republic of China by the *Globe and Mail* in 1977, I came across a dramatic and darkly amusing economic parallel to this phenomenon. It was during 1978, when Communist China was emerging from the devastating Cultural Revolution and Taiwan was adjusting to withdrawal of recognition (as the "official" China) by the United States. Inspecting a former commune in the Canton area of south China, I was fascinated to see how quickly peasant farmers grabbed the new (Communist) government initiative to farm their own small fields (of about one acre), recently returned to them, as well as pocketing their own profits and deciding what the next crop would be, based on their own estimate of what the market wanted. Over in Taiwan, at the same time, the (capitalist) Kuomintang regime was dealing with agricultural woes (declining labour force, random and ill-advised crops) by forcing farmers to pull down their fences on their small allotments (of about one acre), take forced loans from the state to buy mechanical farm equipment, and give a portion of their earnings to the ministry of agriculture. The only thing missing on both sides of the Strait of Formosa was tea with Alice and the Mad Hatter.

decade on earth. "When I look at all the 'isms' I have studied or even believed in," she said to me once a couple of years ago, "the only ism that seems to make any real and lasting sense is 'who'd-have-thought-ism.' We see the world in one strong light, then two airplanes crash into office buildings, and then — *poof!* — suddenly everything is changed. Who'd have thought? For decades, horrible and apocalyptic bloodshed is predicted as the final conclusion to apartheid in South Africa, and then one man is freed from prison and suddenly there is a whole new equation. Who'd have thought?"[64]

For at least twenty-five years, a considerable faction amongst the commentariat and political class of Canada has predicted the end of the monarchy in Canada. Every time a royal visit approached, newspapers and radio and television programmes would start sprouting "experts" and commentators who would blow their little whistles and call "time out" or "game over" for this strange

---

64   Ursula Franklin had her own royal moment a few years ago. During the Golden Jubilee tour of Canada by Queen Elizabeth and Prince Philip in 2002, the Duke of Edinburgh came to Massey College in Toronto, where he had agreed to become the first honorary Senior Fellow. In a simple but quite moving ceremony, he was "gowned" by the College's two most illustrious Senior Fellows: Professor Franklin and Nobel Laureate Professor John Polanyi. Polanyi later observed that the event had placed "our small college in the pathway of history," and Ursula, typically, said Prince Philip had caused a good occasion "to come together and think of something other than ourselves."

association with a "foreign head of state." Polls (of the cheaper variety) would be trotted out to prove all this, but polls these days are usually put together by "pollstergeists" (a useful Marshall McLuhan term) and are as fickle as the last promise you heard from a politician. So what happens? It turns out nothing is inevitable. All of a sudden a government pays attention to the role of the Sovereign and gives her half a chance to shine, and some of the biggest crowds in our history turn out on Parliament Hill in 2010 to celebrate "Canada Day." Suddenly, people remember how great our venerable Sovereign has been, how loyal and steadfast and true; how amazing her eldest son's endurance and contributions have already been; and then into the equation comes her grandson William with his bride and Canada falls in love with them and the storyline has changed from one of neglect to renewed enthusiasm. Who'd have thought?

THE CENTRAL PROBLEM in championing the Crown in Canada and our Royal Family over the past quarter-century — a problem I have not yet really solved in this book — is that the championing has been primarily apologetic, either overtly or subtly. If I have to use a verbal sledgehammer to get the essential decency of Prince Charles across, it is because of the massive corrosion that has accumulated to his name and endeavour. Similarly, if I'm going overboard in showing the history of royal connections in Canada from place names and institutions right across the country, it is because people simply forget how those names came to be: for too many decades, governments and schools let our constitutional monarchy slide from public view until many of us became embarrassed to have a "foreign" head of state, embarrassed by the very mention of the world "royal." Most of our academic and popular historians have let us down miserably for a variety of reasons, and the primary and high school teachers who are supposed to inculcate Canadian history in young Canadians are their willing accomplices/victims. To defend what was once taken for granted and is now assumed to be on the way out produces defensiveness, apology, and — too often — silence.

I do not want to end apologetically, defensively, or silently, however. Instead I want to try to encapsulate what it is about the Crown in Canada that defies rational defence or attack, why it is an overall good, and why we should be doing everything clever or sensible (or both) to protect and preserve it for the sake and benefit of our children and children's children. It is rather mystical stuff I am talking about: mystical and complex. The outstanding French-Canadian historian and Jesuit academic Père Jacques Monet identified it precisely when he wrote about the generic Sovereign of Canada that a king is a king "not because he is well-educated, not because of his influence, not because he is a successful politician, not because he belongs to a particular creed or to a national group. He is king because he was born to be king . . . The king is himself; and it is as the person that he is, that he is king. In proclaiming him to be their sovereign for no other reason than his own self, Canadians emphasize the truth that each one of his subjects also has intrinsic transcendent value each in his own."

That was the theme that Ralph Heintzman, then the editor of the *Journal of Canadian Studies*, took when he celebrated the Canadian Crown on the occasion of the Queen's Silver Jubilee in 1977. It happened also to be the tenth anniversary of the creation of the Order of Canada, by which Canada acknowledges excellence amongst its citizenry, as well as the thirtieth anniversary of the granting of the Letters Patent of 1947, the final step in the gradual delegation of powers from the Sovereign to her appointed representatives at Rideau

Hall,[65] and last but far from least, the twenty-fifth an-niversary of the appointment of the first Canadian governor general, Vincent Massey, in 1952.

Heintzman's essay is one of the finest forays into contemporary writing on the monarchy.[66] Apart from its lucidity of style and generosity of spirit, the essay shows his understanding of the profoundly spiritual nature of the Crown, and that's what makes it so in-sightful. This is the same man, an historian of French Canada and an outstanding public official, who went on

---

[65]   There remains constitutional and political controversy surround-ing the official interpretation of the Letters Patent, which were adopted by King George VI in 1947. In "Myth and Misunderstanding," by Dr. Christopher McCreery, one of Canada's leading experts on the office of the governor general and the honours system itself, issue is taken with two former governors general (Adrienne Clarkson and Michaëlle Jean) who have publicly interpreted this act to mean that the final authority on all matters in Canada was transferred definitively to the governor gen-eral. For the most part, according to McCreery, the Letters Patent merely formalized what was already practice, and he quotes former Prime Min-ister Louis St. Laurent, then the minister of external affairs and "the main architect" of the Letters Patent, that the new understanding and revisions were not in any way "revolutionary or startling . . . [but] serve to bring the law abreast of the present constitutional position and practice." This is some distance from Madame Jean's proclamation in 2009 that she was head of state, after which she had to suffer the embarrassment of being corrected by the prime minister and reminded that she represented the head of state, who was — *surprise, surprise* — still the Queen.

[66]   Other wise writers are listed in the Bibliography, but I am happy particularly to acknowledge here fine scholars and public servants like David Smith, Peter Russell, and Eugene Forsey.

to win the coveted Vanier Medal in 2006 (the highest honour awarded in Canada's public administration), an award named after our most spiritual governor general. At one point in the essay, Heintzman quotes the Canadian Irishman Thomas D'Arcy McGee, a Father of Confederation, who asserted that the virtues of reverence and love that distinguish family life at its best ought to serve as the foundation of the new Canadian nation. McGee wrote, says Heintzman, "that the same virtues which feed and nourish filial affection and conjugal peace in domestic life are essential to uphold civic authority, and these are the virtues on which the monarchical form of government alone can be maintained."

Heintzman's full argument is profound, and I can't really do it justice here except to crib the wonderful section I need to complete the point which he makes far better than I could:

> The idea of the Crown, stated very simply, is that the people is not sovereign. But this simple idea must be carefully interpreted if it is to be properly understood. In the first place, one must ask: what is sovereignty? That, too, can be answered relatively simply: sovereignty is that power than which nothing is higher. The idea of the Crown, then, is that the ultimate source of authority is not to be located in the people

but in something higher, something that is above the people and to which they owe allegiance.

The matter cannot be left there, however. One must hasten to expand the argument in order to point out what this idea of the Crown does not mean, as well as what it does. It does not mean that the people is not free to do as it wishes. In a constitutional monarchy such as our own — which is the only kind worth talking about — the sovereign power may have its source above the people, but the power is exercised by the people and can do only what they themselves have decided upon. A country like Canada where the source of authority is held to be outside the people is no less free than a country like the United States where the people itself is declared to be the source of sovereignty. In fact Canadians have often felt that they enjoyed more true freedom than their neighbours. "We have a free Queen over a free people," John A. Macdonald used to say, "governed by the principles of equity, the principles of religion, the principles of morality — which a fierce democracy never has had and never will have."

If the idea of the Crown — that the people is not sovereign — does not mean that they are not self-governing, what does it mean? If Canadians enjoy self-government to the same degree as Americans, why should they bother to maintain a very different constitutional fiction at the centre of their theory of the state? There are two answers to this question, the first of which has to do with the "practical" virtues of the Crown emphasized by Frank MacKinnon: the need to separate the head of government from the head of state, to keep the politicians in their place, to avoid the partisan character of republican heads of state, etc. There is, however, another kind of answer which has rather more to do with the principles of equity, religion, and morality mentioned by John A. The symbolic assertion that sovereign authority proceeds from a source above us reminds us that, while we are indeed free to act as we wish, we *ought* nevertheless to act in certain ways rather than others: while there is nothing to stop us from doing any foolish thing we choose, there are nevertheless certain principles, higher than our own petty desires, to which we owe allegiance, and which we neglect or abuse at our peril.

Heintzman is at the absolute core of this crucial issue. I actually do not think the vast majority of Canadians think of themselves as living under a monarchy, nor do I think they in any way consider that they live in a republic or a quasi-republic, or want to. To most Canadian ears, both "monarchy" and "republic" sound weird. "Crown" is what sounds right. It is under the Crown that our rights and freedoms have been enshrined. It is under the Crown that our politicians govern. It is under the Crown that our judges and prosecutors and defenders in the justice system operate.

We all live in this wonderfully eccentric federation that somehow seems to work, and wittingly or unwittingly, the country is united by the notion of the Crown just as much as it is by winter, hockey, medicare, and Molson Canadian. The Crown infuses our history and geography, our daily legislative practice, our institutions, and our psyche.

It is wonderful that Elizabeth II, as the heir to the throne we have retained, is such a selfless, duty-bound, devoted person, and not — as she famously pointed out — "a fair-weather friend."[67] The charge that she is a

---

[67]   This footnote has nothing whatsoever to do with fair-weather friends, because you, dear reader, have followed me all the way to these final pages. Instead, it is a final royal and viceregal trivia quiz, and there is a reward for tolerating so many footnotes. Here's the challenge: name two geographical locations and one institution in each province named after any member of the royal family. That means THREE names with royal family connections in each province — 30 names in all. PLUS: I want you also to identify ONE geographical location or institution from each province named after a governor general — ten names in all. Send your 40 answers to me, John Fraser, c/o House of Anansi Press, 110 Spadina Avenue, Suite 801, Toronto, Ontario, M5V 2K4, Canada. The first three accurate answers received and opened by me will get prizes: First Prize is dinner at Massey College with the Senior and Junior Fellows; Second Prize is a bottle of college port; Third Prize is a book of my choosing. All entries will get a somewhat offbeat royal Canadian token of appreciation from the author. This competition, as they say, concludes on June 30, 2012. And, for heaven's sake: *God save the Queen!*

"foreign" head of state doesn't fly, at least to anyone who has looked at it seriously. Indeed, of late, it could almost be said that Britain has something verging on a "foreign" head of state as that increasingly challenged nation starts learning the rigors of a federal system (Scotland is leading the campaign with a Quebec-like flexing of its muscles, while Wales and Northern Ireland look set to become the Alberta and Newfoundland of a Britain that is not so "great" at all anymore). The House of Lords is more and more giving the appearance of the Canadian Senate, and the number of study groups coming from Britain to Canada to study our multicultural and multi-racial successes increases exponentially every year.

Our Queen knew all this from some time ago. Our Queen, acting as their Queen, may already have proffered advice based on the Canadian experience to her government leaders and officials. I personally think they are very lucky over there to have the advice and experience of *our* Queen.

If we agree with this notion, then, that our Queen is our Queen, then the hope for the years to come is that Canadians stop apologizing for her and for the institution she represents, that we celebrate it in the same spirit we celebrated Canada Day with the Queen in 2010 and the royal tour of the Duke and Duchess of Cambridge in

2011. The Queen's much put-upon heir, Prince Charles, is prepared to go along with this script, and because he is a good man whose intentions are altruistic and noble, we are lucky in him too. Ditto for his son, the still blameless Prince William, who in his youth constitutionally enfranchises the young people of this country as no politician can do, not even Justin Trudeau or the members of the NDP Quebec caucus, as important as their contributions are too.

Our Queen is the latest link in a long golden chain that connects the Canadian story. The mystery and magic behind our constitutional arrangements are all tied to an hereditary monarchy. That is the real secret of the Crown. It is our past, which if denied will confound our future; it is our dignity, which if cast carelessly aside will make us a crasser people; it is the protection of our rights, which if abandoned could lead to demagogic manipulation or excess. Most important of all, the Crown defines our uniqueness and is evidence of a mature community that can carry forward its history and heritage and uniqueness with pride. We have a Queen who can rule our hearts if we let her, but who leaves our minds to wander and speculate wherever they will. That is not at all a secret for anyone with eyes to see and ears to hear. It is also the most tangible reality of the Crown today, and that's why, in closing, I say God bless her, and thank her, and longer still may she reign over us, as happy and glorious as it is possible to be in this ever-changing, troublesome world.

NOTES

PROLOGUE: *Why Secret?*

The epigraph comes from a speech by the Queen in Gatineau, Quebec, quoted in the Canadian Press, October 12, 2002.

Michael Bliss's opinion on young Canadians' attitude towards the Monarchy was stated during a debate with the author on the future of the Monarchy in Canada, held at the Royal Ontario Museum, Toronto, on January 21, 2011.

Prime Minister Jean Chrétien's pungent defence of the Monarchy through his interpretation of French-Canadian history (Footnote 5) was stated on April 23, 1994, and quoted from his memoir: Chrétien, Jean. *My Years as Prime Minister.* Toronto: Knopf, 2008. Page 248.

CHAPTER ONE: *The Marriage of a Prince*

The first epigraph is from "Le Canada, une monarchie constitutionnelle," an illustrated brochure published by the Senate of Canada.

The second epigraph is from the *National Post*, June 1, 2011. Page 1.

Walter Bagehot's quote, "A princely marriage is the brilliant edition of a universal fact, and as such, it rivets mankind," is from: Bagehot, Walter. *The English Constitution, 1867*. London: Oxford University Press, 1991. Page 187.

The quote from Jeremy Paxman on royalty and mass media is from: Paxman, Jeremy. *On Royalty*. London: Viking, 2006. Pages 148 and 182.

The quote from Will Self on the Monarchy infantilising the public is from: Self, Will. "Do We Want a Monarchy?" *Prospect*, April 2011.

The quotes from William IV on first landing in Canada in Newfoundland and Quebec, and on his meeting with the First Nations, are from: Zeigler, Philip. *King William IV*. London: Cassell, 1989. Pages 89, 92, and 97.

The article on Étienne Boisvert, the young Quebecois monarchist, is from: Perreaux, Les. "Dieu protège la reine, says young Quebecker." *Globe and Mail*, June 2, 2011.

CHAPTER TWO: *Tribal Monarchy and Local Royalty*

The epigraph is from: Paxman, Jeremy. *On Royalty*. London: Viking, 2006. Page 177.

Claude Bissell's comment on Vincent Massey (Footnote 25) is from: Bissell, Claude. *The Imperial Canadian: Vincent Massey in Office*. Toronto: University of Toronto Press, 1986. Page 128.

Ken Wiwa's comment on Adrienne Clarkson's appointment to the office of governor general (Footnote 28) is from: Wiwa, Ken. *Globe and Mail*, February 1, 2003.

Adrienne Clarkson's "Eulogy for Canada's Unknown Soldier" is from the official Governor General of Canada website: http://archive.gg.ca.

The description of the King-Byng Affair (Footnote 29) is from: http://en.wikipedia.org/wiki/King-Byng_Affair.

Margaret Wente's comment on Hilary Weston's appointment as lieutenant governor of Ontario (Footnote 31), as well as her praise for her tenure, is from: Weston, Hilary. *No Ordinary Time: My Years as Ontario's Lieutenant Governor*. Toronto: Whitfield Editions, 2007. Page 12.

Hilary Weston's summary of the symbolic importance of the position of lieutenant governor is from: *Ibid*. Page 104.

CHAPTER THREE: *King Charles III of Canada?*

The epigraph is from: Milne, A. A. "Buckingham Palace." *When We Were Very Young*. London: Methuen, 1921.

Queen Elizabeth's comment on Prince Philip is from: Queen Elizabeth II. Speech to the Guildhall, 1997, quoted in the *Daily Telegraph*, November 20, 2007.

The article on Prince Philip standing by Queen Elizabeth II for six decades is from: "True Welfare." *Spectator*, June 11, 2011.

The excerpt from *Henry V* (Footnote 41) is from: Shakespeare, William. *Henry V*, Act 4, Scene i. New York: Signet Classics, 1998.

Max Hastings's "landmark" essay is from: Hastings, Max. "Why Prince Charles Is Too Dangerous to Be King: In a landmark essay Max Hastings tells why this increasingly eccentric royal could imperil the monarchy." *Daily Mail*, December 18, 2010.

Doug Saunders's comment on Prince Charles's work *Harmony*

is from: Saunders, Doug. "Britain's Crisis of Succession: Charles and the Story Behind the Royal Wedding." *Globe and Mail*, April 22, 2011.

The excerpt on new-age medicine (Footnote 42) is from: Freedman, David H. "The Triumph of New-Age Medicine." *Atlantic*, July/August 2011.

Michael Valpy's comments on Prince William and Catherine Middleton, and on Prince Charles as king, are from: Valpy, Michael. "Will Charles Make a Good King? Yes." *Globe and Mail*, April 29, 2011.

The excerpts from Prince Charles in the 1994 British Independent Television documentary are quoted in: Dimbleby, Jonathan. *The Prince of Wales: A Biography*. Toronto: Doubleday Canada, 1994. Page 332.

Archbishop Carey's correction of Prince Charles's comments on "Defender of Faith" is from: *Ibid*. Page 342.

Prince Charles's feelings on religion (Footnote 44) are from: *Ibid*. Page 342.

Prince Charles's speech at the 250th anniversary of the Board of Deputies of British Jews at the historic Guildhall is quoted from the official website of the British Monarchy: www.royal.gov.uk.

Prince Charles's January 21, 1993, letter to Tom Shebbeare, then the director of the Prince's Trust, is from: Dimbleby, Jonathan. *The Prince of Wales: A Biography*. Toronto: Doubleday Canada, 1994. Page 376.

CHAPTER FOUR: *Long to Reign Over Us*

The epigraph is from the Canadian Monarchist Online: http://home.interlog.com/~rakhshan/pquotes.html.

Excerpts from Anna Brownell Jameson are from: Jameson, Anna Brownell. *Winter Studies and Summer Rambles in Canada* (1836). Toronto: McClelland & Stewart, 2009. Page 139.

Wilfrid Laurier's comment on Queen Victoria is from: Schull, Joseph. *Laurier: The First Canadian*. Toronto: Macmillan of Canada, 1965. Page 571.

Arthur Bousfield and Garry Toffoli's description of King Edward at his Alberta ranch is from: Bousfield, Arthur, and Garry Toffoli. *Royal Tours, 1786–2010: Home to Canada*. Toronto: Dundurn Press, 2010. Page 62.

Queen Elizabeth's twenty-first-birthday radio broadcast from South Africa is from: Pimlott, Ben. *The Queen: A Biography of Elizabeth II*. London: HarperCollins, 1996. Page 224.

Lord Altrincham's description of the Queen (Footnote 55) is from: *Ibid.* Page 301.

The description of the July 9, 1982, break-in at the Queen's residence (Footnote 58) is from: *Ibid.* Page 580.

The excerpt from Queen Elizabeth's 1992 speech is from the official website of the British Monarchy: www.royal.gov.uk.

CHAPTER FIVE: *The Once and Future Crown*

The epigraph by Ted Hughes is from the official website of the British Monarchy: www.royal.gov.uk.

The quote from Samuel Johnson (Footnote 64) is from: Johnson, Samuel. *The Works of Samuel Johnson*, Vol. 14. Troy, New York: Parfracts & Company, 1913. Page 98.

Dr. Christopher McCreery's comment on the Letters Patent (Footnote 69) is from: McCreery, Christopher. *The Order of Canada: Its Origins, History, and Development*. Toronto: Dundurn Press, 2006. Page 15.

Ralph Heintzman's essay is from: Heintzman, Ralph. "The Meaning of Monarchy." *Journal of Canadian Studies*, Vol. 12, No. 4 (Summer 1977). Page 2.

BIBLIOGRAPHY

Allison, Ronald, and Sarah Riddell, eds. *The Royal Encyclopedia*. London: Macmillan Press, 1999.

Bagehot, Walter. *The English Constitution, 1867*. London: Oxford University Press, 1991.

Bissell, Claude. *The Imperial Canadian: Vincent Massey in Office*. Toronto: University of Toronto Press, 1986.

Bousfield, Arthur, and Garry Toffoli. *Royal Tours, 1786–2010: Home to Canada*. Toronto: Dundurn Press, 2010.

Boyce, Peter. *The Queen's Other Realms: The Crown and Its Legacy in Australia, Canada and New Zealand*. Sydney: The Federation Press, 2009

Bradford, Sarah. *King George VI*. London: Weidenfeld & Nicolson, 1989.

Channon, Sir Henry. *Chips: The Diaries of Sir Henry Channon*. London: Weidenfeld & Nicolson, 1967.

Charles, Prince of Wales. *Charles in His Own Words*. London: W. H. Allen, 1981.

Charles, Prince of Wales. *Harmony: A New Way of Looking at Our World*. London: HarperCollins, 2011.

Chrétien, Jean. *My Years as Prime Minister*. Toronto: Knopf, 2008.

Clarkson, Adrienne. *Heart Matters*. Toronto: Penguin Books, 2007.

Coady, Mary Frances. *George and Pauline Vanier: Portrait of a Couple*. Montreal: McGill-Queen's University Press, 2011.

Crawford, Marion. *The Little Princesses*. London: Cassell and Company, 1950.

Crawford, Marion. *Queen Elizabeth II*. London: George Newnes, 1952.

Dimbleby, Jonathan. *The Prince of Wales: A Biography*. Toronto: Doubleday Canada, 1994.

Edward, Duke of Windsor. *A King's Story: The Memories of the Duke of Windsor*. New York: Thomas Allen, 1951.

Forsey, Eugene A. *How Canadians Govern Themselves.* Ottawa: Government of Canada Publications, 2005.

Fraser, John. *Eminent Canadians: Candid Tales of Then and Now.* Toronto: McClelland & Stewart, 2000.

Halpenny, Francess G., and Jean Hamelin, eds. *Dictionary of Canadian Biography: Index for Volumes I to XII, 1000 to 1900.* Toronto: University of Toronto Press, 1991.

Hobsbawm, Eric, and Terence Ranger, eds. *The Invention of Tradition.* Cambridge: Canto Press, 1983.

Jackson, D. Michael. *The Canadian Monarchy in Saskatchewan.* Regina: Government of Saskatchewan Publications, 1990.

Jameson, Anna Brownell. *Winter Studies and Summer Rambles in Canada* (1836). Toronto: McClelland & Stewart, 2009.

Johnson, Samuel. *The Works of Samuel Johnson,* Volume 14. Troy, New York: Parfraets & Company, 1913.

Longford, Elizabeth, ed. *The Oxford Book of Royal Anecdotes.* London: Oxford University Press, 1988.

MacLeod, Kevin S. *A Crown of Maples: Constitutional Monarchy in Canada*. Ottawa: Government of Canada Publications, 2008

McCreery, Christopher. *The Canadian Honours System*. Toronto: Dundurn Press, 2005.

McCreery, Christopher. *The Order of Canada: Its Origins, History, and Development*. Toronto: Dundurn Press, 2006.

McWhinney, Edward. *The Governor General and the Prime Ministers*. Vancouver: Ronsdale Press, 2005.

Monet, Jacques. *The Canadian Crown*. Toronto: Clarke & Company, 1979.

Nicholson, Harold. *King George V*. London: Constable, 1952.

Paxman, Jeremy. *On Royalty*. London: Viking Books, 2006.

Pimlott, Ben. *The Queen: A Biography of Elizabeth II*. London: HarperCollins Publishers, 1996.

Sarah, Duchess of York, with Jeff Coplin. *My Story*. London: Simon & Schuster, 1996.

Schull, Joseph. *Laurier: The First Canadian.* Toronto: Macmillan of Canada, 1965.

Strachey, Lytton. *Queen Victoria.* London: Penguin Books, 2000.

Tidridge, Nathan. *Canada's Constitutional Monarchy.* Toronto: Dundurn Press, 2011.

Victoria, Queen of Great Britain and Empress of India. *Queen Victoria's Highland Journals.* Selected and edited by Christopher Hibbert. London: Penguin Books, 1985.

Weston, Hilary. *No Ordinary Time: My Years as Ontario's Lieutenant Governor.* Toronto: Whitfield Editions, 2007

Zeigler, Philip. *Crown and People.* London: Collins, 1978.

Zeigler, Philip. *King William IV.* London: Cassell, 1989.

Zeigler, Philip. *King Edward VIII.* Stroud: Sutton Publishing, 1990.

ACKNOWLEDGEMENTS

Some brief parts of this book have appeared in a different form in past issues of *Saturday Night* magazine during my years there as editor (1987 to 1995), and in both the *Globe and Mail* and the *National Post*, where I once worked regularly. As well, a short personal account of the 1953 Coronation appeared in a different form in my book *Eminent Canadians: Candid Tales of Then and Now* (McClelland & Stewart). Also, in the late spring of 2011, *Maclean's* commissioned me to write eight essays on Crown and Country from the period leading up to the wedding of Prince William and Catherine Middleton until after their first tour together across Canada. Some of that material has been incorporated into the overall text. I am grateful for the opportunities all those publications, as well as three British publications (*The Spectator*, the *Daily Telegraph*, and the *Daily Mail*), provided through the Internet to quote from them. I am also grateful for the specific permission of

Jonathan Dimbleby and Doubleday Canada to quote from his 1994 biography of Prince Charles (*The Prince of Wales: A Life*), and HarperCollins and the literary estate of the late Ben Pimlott for some quotes from his 1996 biography of the Queen (*The Queen: A Biography of Elizabeth II*).

At the House of Anansi, I owe huge debts to everyone, but especially to Sarah MacLachlan (president), Scott Griffin (saviour), Meredith Dees (who did all the photo and image research), and — most of all — the sensitive, brilliant editing of a messy manuscript by Janie Yoon.

In the course of writing this book, and in the long period leading up to it, I have received all sorts of practical help or insight (or both), for which I am grateful. This assistance has been as wonderful as it has been good-natured and various: from the editors and checkers at *Maclean's* to the Van Tullekan family in Go Home Bay, who provided (hydro) electricity on those days when my (solar) electricity supplies were minimal; to the wonderful staff at Clarence House, the official office of the Prince of Wales (who helped to make coverage of Prince William's marriage to Catherine Middleton so effortless and such fun); and to the Porter's Lodge at Massey College presided over by the redoubtable Senior Porter, Sgt. Elizabeth Hope.

The incomplete list here of gratefully acknowledged assistance of a similarly wide variety (inadvertent and specific, pro- and anti-monarchy, dead and alive) is alphabetical and not at all based on any priority of help rendered, or status. From each of them, as from so many others, I have learned something in one form or another that led, by some sort of intellectual alchemy or osmosis, to this book:

Rosalie Abella, the late John Black Aird, Lincoln Alexander, Jamie Anderson, Patsy Anderson, the late Peter Anderson, Aubie Angel, Sally Armstrong, Margaret Atwood, Dan Avnon, Andrew Baines, Cornelia Baines, the late St. Clair Balfour, the late June Barrett, James Bartleman, Mikhail Baryshnikov, the late John Bassett, Isabel Bassett, Douglas Bell, Avie Bennett, Richard Berthelsen, Angud Bhalla, Suresh Bhalla, Andrew Binkley, Harriet Binkley, Grant Bishop, Lord Black, Christie Blatchford, Elizabeth Bliss, Molly Blyth, Henry Borden, Lisa Balfour Bowen, Walter Bowen, Cathrin Bradbury, Diana Bradshaw, the late Richard Bradshaw, Alan Broadbent, the late Erik Bruhn, Ann Brumell, Brendy Bury, the late Esmond Butler, Edmund Cape, King Carl XVI Gustaf of Sweden, James Carley, Graydon Carter, David Campbell, Kim Campbell, Nanda

Cassuci-Bryne, Greg Cerson, Jean Charest, the late Barrie Ramsey Chavel, James Chavel, Matthew Chavel, Jean Chrétien, Jill Clark, Joe Clark, Tom Clark, Austin Clarke, Adrienne Clarkson, Anne Collins, Michael Cooke, Jack Costello, Andrew Coyne, the late A. H. Crosbie, Andrea Crosbie, the late Gertrude Crosbie, Jane Crosbie, John Crosbie, William Crosbie, Brenda Davies, the late Robertson Davies, William Davis, Thomas Delworth, Jack Diamond, the late Barbara Forrester Dickinson, the late Catherine Dickinson, the late John Diefenbaker, Jonathan Dimbleby, John Dirks, the late Richard J. Doyle, Dorothy Dunlop, Stefan Dupré, Danylo Dzwonyk, Frederik Eaton, Noel Edison, Atom Egoyan, Barbara English, Arthur English, Michael Enright, Diane de Fenoyl, Kate Filion, Terence Finlay, Thomas Fitches, Tyler Flatt, the late Eugene Forsey, Allan Fotheringham, Ursula Franklin, Jane Freeman, David Frum, Robert Fulford, Kelly Gale, George Galt, Judith Skelton Grant, John Geiger, Irving Gerstein, Graeme Gibson, Daniel Goldbloom, David Goldbloom, the late Walter Gordon, Allan Gotlieb, Mary Graham, Jack Granatstein, the late George Grant, Charlotte Gray, Rudyard Griffiths, Robin Harris, Wendy Henderson Heasman, Jane Heintzman, Ralph Heintzman, Lisa Henderson, Jane Hilderman, the late Louise Hill, Ernest Hillen, the late Lord Harlow, the late Richard Hatfield, the late Steve Herder, John Honderich, Huang Anlun, J. N. (Pat) Hume, Robert Hyland, Frank Iacobucci, the late Alison Ignatieff, Andrew Ignatieff, the late George Ignatieff, Michael Ignatieff, Eric Jackman, H. N. R. Jackman, Michael Jackson, George Jonas, Serge Joyal, Karen Kain, Patricia Kennedy, Jason Kenny, Craig Kielburger, Baron King, Frank King, Norma King, Ralph King, the late Lincoln Kirstein, Marie Korey, Michael Laine, Peter Latka, Mary Jo Leddy, Michael Levine, Myles Leslie, Joyce Lewis, Peter Lewis, Lord Linley, the late Earl of Longford, Patrick Luciani, Anna Luengo, Anthony Luengo, Joan MacCallum, Christopher MacDonald, P. J. MacDougall, Kevin Macleod, Margaret MacMillan, Brian Maloney, Preston Manning, Dow Marmur, Lorna Marsden, the late Hart Massey, John Massey, the late Vincent Massey, Kenneth McCarter, Christopher McCreery, Barbara McDougall, Ivan McFarlane, the late Pauline McGibbon, Carolyn McIntire-Smyth, the late Norah Michener, the late Roland Michener, Noam Miller, Jacques Monet, the late Barbara Moon, Charles Moore, Brian Mulroney, Darlene Naranjo, David Naylor, Peter C. Newman, Alastair Niven, Ray Novak, Amy Nugent, the late Fabian O'Dea, Shane O'Dea, Sir Christopher Ondaatje, Lady Ondaatje, David Onley, James Orbinsky, the late Bernard Ostry, Sylvia Ostry, Mark Ozon, Cheryl Palmer, Jacques Parizeau, Roger Parkinson, Charles Pascal, Lord Patten, Anthony Pawson, the late E. B. (Bill) Pearce, the late L. B. Pearson, John Perlin, Susan Perren, David Peterson, Heather Peterson, James Peterson, Prince Philip, John Polanyi, Lord Polwarth, Julian Porter, the late Jane Poulson, Neville Poy, Rob Prichard, Jack Rabinovich, Bob Rae, David Reibetanz, Jonathan Reid, Florence Richler, the late Mordecai Richler, Noah Richler, Nancy Ruth, Ann Saddlemyer, Richard Sadleir, John Ralston Saul, the late Jeanne Sauvé, Robin Sears, Norma Sebenyi, Hugh Segal, the late Pierre Sévigny, Geraldine Sharpe, William Shawcross, Gerry Sheff, Brigitte Shim, Jeffrey Simpson, the late Patwant Singh, Bengt Skoggard, Joey Slinger, the late Joseph R. Smallwood, Alexander McCall Smith, Mark Smith, Harley Smyth, the late C. P. Snow, Nancy Southam, John Stackhouse, Janice Stein, Geoffrey Stevens, Amy Stewart, Andrew Stewart, Nalini Stewart, Tim Stewart, Douglas Stoute, Sarmishtra Subramanian, Jennifer Surridge, Queen Sylvia, Dianna Symonds, Christine Symons, Thomas Symons, Norma Szebenyi, Veronica Tennant, Lady Thatcher, the late Lord Thomson, R. H. Thomson, Cindy Caron Thorburn, William Thorsell, Nathan Tidridge, Vincent Tovell, Patricia Treble, the late

Pierre Trudeau, John Turner, Desmond Tutu, Jean Vanier, Ian Webb, Norman Webster, Galen Weston, Hilary Weston, the late Herbert Whittaker, Kenneth Whyte, Richard Winter, Rose Wolfe, Adam Zimmerman, Moses Znaimer.

Actually, I'm wrong. The priority of importance begins here. To the remarkable women in my life: to Elizabeth Scott MacCallum; to Jessie, Kate, and Clara Fraser, my deepest love and thanks. To my late and hugely missed sister, Barrie Chavel, my unceasing gratitude. (*Okay, then,* and also to Molly Bloom, a wonderful dog who died during the writing of this book, leaving us all without complaint and loyal to the end. And to Maddy, her successor, who came to us afterwards and soothed me during all the editing, rewriting, fact-checking, and other ordeals.)

INDEX

Adonis, Andrew, Lord, 21
Alexandra, Queen, 112, 113f38
Altrincham, Lord, 168, 168f53
An Uncommon Reader (Bennett),
    163–64
Andrew, Prince, 7, 11, 171
Anne, Princess (the Princess
    Royal), 7, 16, 171
Anne, Queen, 28f15
Atwood, Margaret, 144
Australia
    Commonwealth prime minis-
       ters' conference, 94–95
    referendum on monarchy,
       xx–xxi, 171
automatic deference, and tribal
    monarchy, 19–20

Bagehot, Walter, 3, 10, 22, 92
Bartleman, James, 86–87
Becket, Thomas, 129
Bennett, Alan, *An Uncommon
    Reader,* 163–64
Berthelson, Richard, 85
Berton, Pierre, 35
Bissell, Claude, on Vincent

Massey, 69f25
Black, Conrad, 55, 118
Blair, Tony, 5
Bliss, Michael, xiii, xvi
    Canadian nationalism, 41–42
    on monarchy, and young
       Canadians, xv
    monarchy debate, xxii–xxiv
Board of Deputies of British Jews
    "Unity through Diversity"
       speech, 131–32
Boisvert, Étienne, 43–44
Bousfield, Arthur, 162f49
Brandreth, Gyles, 113f38
Brault, Jacques, *Suite Fraternelle,*
    76
Brennan, Richard, 83
Brown, Gordon, 5
"Buckingham Palace" (Milne), 98
Burmese (horse), 170, 170f55

Campbell, Kim, 93
Canada
    British monarchy as Canadian
       "Crown", 13–14, 14f11, 202–5
    as constitutional monarchy,

Charles, 110, 111–12
Pascal, Blaise, 133
Paxman, Jeremy
on meeting the Queen, 155–56
On Royalty, 15, 48
Pearson, Lester, 40–41
Philip, Prince, Duke of
Edinburgh
2010 Canada Day celebration,
xxi
at Massey College, 103–4, 106,
194f64
media awareness, 99–107,
99–100f34
in People's Republic of China,
102
and Princess Diana, 103
Royal Family of Canada, 13–14
Pimlott, Ben, 40–41, 170f56
Polanyi, John, 194f64
pollstergeists, and end of monarchy, 195
Prince's Trust, 133–34f44
privacy, and media attention, 33,
99–107, 99–100f34, 109–10
The Private Capital (Gwyn),
154–55

Quebec
and provincial unanimity for
republic, xix–xx
Quiet Revolution, 34, 39–41,
45
religion, and acceptance of
monarchy, xxf5, 38–39
and role of monarchy in
Canada, 36–39
Truncheon Saturday, 39–41,
171

The Queen (film), 163
The Queen (Pimlott, biography),
170f56
quiz, royal trivia, 202f67

Riel, Louis, 151
"Right Royal" style of governor
general, 69–70, 71f27
Rotstein, Abraham, 103
Royal 22nd Regiment, 62
royal scarecrows, 12–13, 14–15
royal tours
Charles and Camilla, 137–38
Charles and Diana, 25, 112
Elizabeth II and Prince Philip,
xxi, 28–29, 103–4, 106,
194f64, 195
George VI and Elizabeth
(Queen Mother), 23, 29
Golden Jubilee of Elizabeth II,
x, 102
People's Republic of China, 102
Queen Mother, 89
success of, and anti-monar-
chists, 21
William and Catherine, 17–18,
23–25, 28
William IV (son of George III),
25–27
Russell, Peter, 79

Saul, John Ralston, 43, 78, 81, 144
Saunders, Doug, 120–21
Sauvé, Jeanne, 71f27, 93
Schreyer, Edward, xv, 71f27
Self, Will
monarchy, and infantilisation
of public, 21, 21f13
Shaughnessy, Baron, 150

235

JOHN FRASER is a Canadian journalist, author, and academic, who has served as Master of Massey College at the University of Toronto since 1995. As a journalist, he has received multiple national awards, and his work has been published in many of the leading international journals and newspapers, including the *New York Times*, the *Washington Post*, the *New Republic*, the *Christian Science Monitor*, *Maclean's*, the *Guardian*, the *Spectator*, the *Daily Telegraph*, *Paris Match*, and the *New Republic*. He is the author of nine works of nonfiction and one novel. He lives in Toronto.